Soccer – Perfect Ball Control

Acknowledgement:

Thank you to Norbert Elgert, Sven Huebscher, Horst Wein, Joerg Amthor and Dr. Gerd Thissen for all the suggestions they have given me in discussions or in collaboration in other projects.

Thanks to Justin Kaiser, Christopher Zeh, Mahmud Aiub, Marcello Lopergolo, Kevin Liebe for sparing the time to pose for the photos in this book.

Peter Schreiner

Peter Schreiner

SOCCER
Perfect Ball Control

Meyer & Meyer Sport

Original title: Fußball – Perfekte Ballbeherrschung
© Meyer & Meyer Verlag, 2009

Translated by Heather Ross

British Library Cataloguing in Publication Data
A catalogue record for this book is available from the British Library

Soccer – Perfect Ball Control
Peter Schreiner
Maidenhead: Meyer & Meyer Sport (UK) Ltd., 2010
ISBN: 978-1-84126-278-9

© 2010 by Meyer & Meyer Sport (UK) Ltd.
Aachen, Adelaide, Auckland, Budapest, Cape Town, Graz, Indianapolis,
Maidenhead, Olten (CH), Singapore, Toronto
Member of the World
Sport Publishers' Association (WSPA)
www.w-s-p-a.org
Printed by: B.O.S.S Druck und Medien GmbH
ISBN: 978-1-84126-278-9
E-Mail: info@m-m-sports.com
www.m-m-sports.com

CONTENTS

INTRODUCTION

The modern game of soccer puts players of all abilities under great pressure from both time and opponents. It is rarely possible to receive the ball calmly and then dribble, pass or shoot at the goal. Only players who have perfect ball control in the most difficult situations can quickly and safely – often on the move – be able to play successful soccer.

Perfect ball control does not just begin when the ball is at the player's foot; it should always be seen in the context of a game situation and an opponent. Well before the first touch of the ball, the player should be preparing to receive it by absorbing information and making split-second judgments as to which move would best suit this particular game scenario (anticipation). His/her decisions and the way he plays as a result determine the success of his

Perfect ball control can therefore be divided into four phases:

1. Preparation for the first touch (perception, release, adopting the body position necessary for the game situation).

2. The first touch.

3. Actions with the ball (dribbling, feints).

4. Final action (pass, cross, shot at the goal).

Phase 1: Preparation for the first touch

In a soccer game, a player takes in many different signals that help him to evaluate the game situation and to play with clever tactics. The player therefore prepares for the first touch so that he can safely control the ball **and** the opponent. This involves adopting an open and game-appropriate body position; his body is balanced and is perfectly prepared for the first touch.

Phase 2: The first touch

The player traps the ball with feeling, controls it and guides it directly to his teammate or takes a shot at the goal. The first touch should always be purposeful. The player prepares the action with the ball and thinks about the direction of the follow-through move.

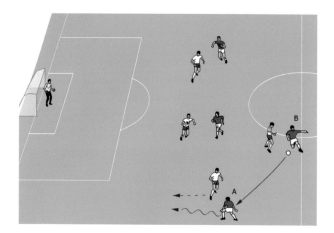

Phase 3: Moves with ball possession

After controlling the ball, the player shields the ball and secures possession of the ball for his team. If a space opens up for the player, he opts to control the ball or tempo dribble with a view to preparing to pass to a teammate or take a shot at the goal. If necessary, he shakes off an opponent with a feint.

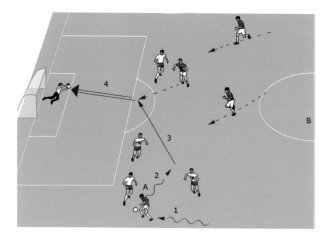

Phase 4: Final action

In the last ball control phase, the player makes a split-second decision as to what to do with the ball next and then puts his decision into practice either alone or with a teammate. A great deal of practice is needed to acquire a feel for the right amount of energy to use when receiving the ball, passing the ball, crossing or shooting at the goal. The ball reacts immediately to the slightest error (e.g. kicking the wrong part of the ball at the wrong time or kicking it too hard) thus leading to the ball being lost. The player must adapt his movements to those of the ball, thus developing a feeling for the ball which is critical for good ball technique.

This book contains basic theories and tried and tested and effective drills which will help your players learn to control their bodies, the ball and the attacking opponent.

1 DEVELOPING AND IMPROVING THE FEEL FOR THE BALL

1.1 Balance – the Key to Perfection with the Ball

Top players like Cristiano Ronaldo and Ronaldinho control the ball at top speed and in extremely pressured situations both on the ground and in the air. This requires outstanding coordination and, in particular, exceptional balance. The player must adjust to the forces that are constantly acting on his/her body. Good physical perception and quick movement control are necessary after jumping, turning and being tackled by opponents.

Top players do not allow themselves to be caught off guard by a tackle, they adapt their movements to the pressure without losing balance.

Problems with their balance also mean problems with the ball!

Lack of balance leads to instability and technical problems. Small deviations, e.g. in the foot placement of the standing leg, make the difference between:

- Fast and safe ball control or losing the ball.
- Accurate diagonal passes or a missed opportunity to counterattack.
- Accurate cross or shots behind the goal.
- Scoring a goal or hitting the post.

Perfect soccer technique starts with the feet, so that drills on soft surfaces are essential for the development of technical precision.

1.2 Perception – the Foundation of Controlled Body Posture and Precise Movements

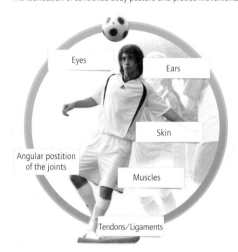

Perception
The foundation of controlled body posture and precise movements

Eyes

Ears

Skin

Angular postition of the joints

Muscles

Tendons/Ligaments

Only players who are able to perceive their surroundings and their bodies quickly and accurately can adapt their physical posture, running and soccer technique to a changing game situation. Perception is therefore a fundamental prerequisite for perfect ball control.

When we talk about perception, we think first of all of the **eyes**, for they receive important visual information about the movement of the ball, opponent and teammates. The **ears** not only receive acoustic signals, such as the whistle, shouting and the noise of the ball, but the inner ear also provides information on the turns and movement speed of our own bodies, which is indispensable for dynamic balance.

Kinesthesia and **proprioception** are required to play technically perfect soccer. **Pressure changes in the skin** inform a player about what an opponent is doing behind his back.

The knowledge of the speed and **angular position of the joints** is necessary for an accurate kicking technique, particularly when the player is watching the ball or the movements of his teammates. Information from the **muscles, tendons and ligaments** complete the player's inner picture of his/her posture, and proper ball control is only possible with quick and accurate inner perception.

Where does balance originate?
* Sense of balance – vestibular apparatus.
* In the muscles and tendons (kinesthetic analyzers), tensions, changes, lengths.
* Posture and startle reflexes guarantee a normal physical posture and balance.

- Tactile analyzers (vibrations, type of surface, depth of impression, sense of posture, spatial awareness).
- Visual analyzers (eyes), anticipation – particularly important in complex movements.
- Processing in central nervous system (coordination of voluntary movements – carrying out targeted movements) – comparison with previous experiences.

Balance drills teach movement stability, postural stability and physical self-confidence, thus leading to better technique.

Postural stability
Physical posture becomes more stable and helps the player to win tackles and to pass the ball accurately or shoot at the goal despite being tackled by an opponent. Experienced players anticipate physical contact and the resulting pressure on the body by an opponent and do not let this unbalance them. This ability is also improved by gaining strength and improving inter- and intramuscular coordination.

Self-confidence
Proprioception training boosts the players' confidence in their own bodies and their bodies' capacity to develop in order to cope with the different demands of the game, particularly where the players' tackling ability is concerned.

How does proprioception training work?
Proprioception training works on the awareness of movements, the position of the joints and muscle tension.

Movement sense
Although players don't see how their legs move, they sense the movement. They control and regulate the desired motion sequence via the movement sense in their joints.

Position sense
The position sense in the joints enables players to, e.g., set the position of their ankle when kicking. They sense the position of their foot and control their kicking technique without looking at their feet. This sense also allows them to perceive and control their body's position in space.

Force sense
Feedback on muscle tension and the muscle tension relationships in the body complements the movement sense of the limbs and the postural sense.

There are three types of balance:

Static Balance
Static balance involves the maintenance and restoration of balance at relative rest or during very slow movement without changing place.

Dynamic Balance
Good dynamic balance is required for jumping and turning and rapid changes of direction.

Object Balance
Object balance involves trying to hold or move an object while balancing it.

The training of balance is an indispensable part of the training program, from kids and young players right up to professionals.

1.3   Practice: Proprioception and Balance Training

1.3.1   Solo Drills with the Ball

Ball on the ground – swinging movements with the foot around the ball (circle, figure eight).

Move the ball on the ground with the foot (left-right or back and forth).

left-right

back and forth

Balancing the ball on the head while stationary.

Juggling the ball (thigh and instep).

1.3.2   Partner Drills with the Ball

Passing on the ground with the **inside of the foot** (left/right).

Passing with the inside of the foot

Standing on one leg (left and right) + **throwing and catching the ball** with both hands (varying distances: from very close to 3 yards away).

Throwing in different directions
- to the chest, over the head.
- to the left and right.
- at knee height.

Catching and throwing

Ball control (chest, thigh, instep, head) + **catching and throwing back.**

Chest   *Thigh*   *Head*

Variation:

Trapping the ball (chest, thigh, instep) + **passing back.**

Volley (inside of the foot, instep, hip turn kick) and **header.**

Variation:

both players head the ball.

Inside   *Header*

1.3.3   Group Drills

Groups of three (one player on the mat, 90°)
Two players take turns in throwing the ball to the partner in the middle. The player in the middle passes the ball back either directly or after controlling it.

Ball control techniques:
chest, thigh, inside, instep.

Passing techniques:
inside, instep, hip turn kick.

Groups of three (one player on the mat, 180°)
The player in the middle turns around 180°.

Ball control:
chest or thigh.

Techniques Pass:
Inside, instep, hip turn kick, head.

Groups of three (all players on the mat)
Three players form a triangle on a mat and pass the ball to each other.

- Throw – header to next player – catch.

- Throw – kick with the inside of the foot (volley) to next player – catch.

- Throw – hip turn kick (volley) to next player – catch.

Variations for advanced players:
- Direct header in a triangle.
- Direct kick with the inside of the foot.
- Juggling in a triangle.

1.3.4   Tackles by an Opponent

In a match, players are constantly subject to forces due to opponents' tackles, which they must quickly absorb and compensate for. Good body perception and quick movement control are necessary for the player to bring the ball safely under control, pass or shoot at the goal. Players must learn to feel this pressure, anticipate it and counteract it in training.

Pass back to partner after trapping the ball (chest, thigh).

Direct pass back to partner (inside of the foot, instep, hip turn kick, head).

1.4   Juggling

1.4.1   Basic Theory

Why is juggling such an important part of soccer training?
- Juggling develops agility and skill with the ball.
- Juggling drills teach players to keep the ball under control in the air with different parts of the body.
- Juggling teaches a feel for the ball (kinesthetic differentiation), which is vital for good ball technique.
- The player learns to coordinate his own movements with those of the ball.
- Juggling develops coordination (balance, linking ability, cognitive ability, responsiveness).
- Juggling improves concentration.

Juggling training objectives
- Juggling with both feet.
- Successive juggling movements, the ball touches the ground as little as possible.
- To develop creativity by varying the use of feet, thighs, chest and head. In solo drills, the player aims to gradually increase the number of times he touches the ball with different parts of his body.

Juggling should not become an end in itself and should be included into the soccer training process, as pure ball jugglers have no chance in fast-paced modern soccer.

1.4.2 Learning to Juggle

1.4.2.1 Balancing

Experts not only juggle the ball perfectly, they are also able to trap it with a part of the body every time and balance it in order to bring the ball to rest and slow its momentum.

Learning stages
- A good preliminary exercise is to start by rolling the ball onto the foot and trapping it with the instep against the shin. The ball must not roll to the side.
- Once the player can balance the ball safely with the instep, he/she should try to trap it by swinging the foot toward the ball and slowing it down, then stopping it briefly before passing it up again. With a little practice it should be possible to trap the ball out of the juggle with the instep and balance it on the foot. A very quick change from one foot to the other is also very impressive.

Developing a feel for the ball
- On the foot.
- On the thigh.
- On the head.
- On the back (shoulders).

Balancing on the shoulders
This drill is particularly different because the player cannot see the ball. Start by placing the ball on the shoulders and concentrate on the feeling that the ball gives you. Next, try to briefly throw the ball up and catch it with the shoulders, with the aid of your head and neck. The ball rolls from the back of the head in a fluid movement down the neck to the shoulders.

1.4.2.2 Solo Drills for Beginners

The following drills develop the player's feel for playing the ball high with predetermined parts of the body. This is easiest if the ball is passed from the hands or thrown to the player.

High throw – thigh

- Throw the ball high, kick up with the thigh and trap it.
- Number of reps:
  10 x right/10 x left/10 times alternating.

Mistakes

- The thigh is not at a 90° angle (L position).
- The ball is thrown too high.
- The upper body is too close to the ball.
- The ball is not controlled when passed or passed to high above the head.
- The standing leg lacks stability and the player wobbles.

High throw – forehead

- Throw the ball with both hands about 1.5 feet above head height.
- Pass and trap the falling ball with the forehead (x 10).

Out of the hand with the instep
- Let the ball drop from the hands or throw it slightly upward.
- Kick the ball up high with the instep before it touches the ground, trap the ball.
- Number of reps: 10 x right/10 x left/10 times alternating.

Juggling with the instep after the ball touches the ground
- Throw the ball up, let it bounce on the ground, kick up high with the instep and then catch it with the hands.
- Each time the ball touches the ground, kick it up with the instep for as long as possible.

1.4.2.3   Solo Drills for Advanced Players

Trapping combinations

The player links touches with the thigh, head and foot in predetermined **sequences of two** and then traps the ball:

- Foot – thigh
- Foot – head
- Head – thigh
- Head – foot
- Thigh – head
- Thigh – foot

The player plays the ball alternately with thigh, head and foot in predetermined

sequences of three:

- Foot – thigh – head
- Foot – head – thigh
- Thigh – head – foot
- Head – thigh – foot

Juggling with ground contact and forward movement

- Play the ball high with the instep while moving forward.
- The ball bounces on the ground once after each touch.

Juggling without the ball touching the ground

The player juggles the ball as often as possible...

- with the instep (right foot only/left foot only/alternating).
- with the thigh (right foot only/left foot only/alternating).
- with the head.
- with the instep, thigh and head as desired.
- with prearranged combinations of instep, thigh and head.

If the ball drops to the ground, the player lifts it with his foot by dragging the ball back with the sole of the foot to give the ball the necessary momentum to roll onto the instep or the toes. The player pulls the ball up in a flowing movement and starts juggling again.

1.4.2.4   Partner and Group Drills

Introduction

It is also a good idea to incorporate the sensitive and controlled lifting of the ball into partner and group situations in order to ensure that the learning process is ongoing, thus bringing the necessary variety, motivation and concentration to the 'fight against gravity.' Elementary juggling skills, acquired via solo drills, are a prerequisite for group and partner drills.

Passing from the hand

- Two players stand opposite each other about 2-4 yards apart and pass the ball back and forth to each other with the instep.
- They trap the ball with the thigh, chest or head.
- The player then takes the ball in his hands and passes it back to his partner with his/her instep.

Passing without catching

- The players pass the ball back and forth to each other with the instep.
- They trap the ball with the thigh or chest.
- They try to pass the ball on without touching it with their hands.
- Variation: before passing the ball back to his partner, the player juggles it a few times with his/her foot, thigh and head.

Juggling in a group and changing places

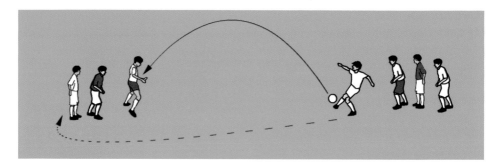

Execution

The first player kicks with the instep to the player opposite him, runs behind the ball and stands with the group opposite. The next player traps the ball quickly with the thigh or chest and passes it after 2-3 juggling touches back to the other side. The players bring their bodies behind the ball when trapping the ball and juggling.

Juggling in a circle

Execution

One player stands in the middle of a circle. Each ball is passed back by the outside players to the player in the middle.

Stage 1

The player in the middle throws the ball; the partner quickly traps it (possibly juggling it 2 or 3 times) and passes it back to the player in the middle.

Stage 2

The player in the middle no longer catches the ball with his hands but traps it with his chest, thigh, foot or head and passes it back to the outside players with his foot.

1.4.2.5 Juggling Competitions

a) Soccer tennis without a Net – 1v1

The game 'soccer tennis without a net' is easy to understand and organize and is highly effective – especially for technical training. It can be done on the playing field or on any free playing surface as an individual or team tournament competition.

Training emphases
- Accurate and measured kicking of the ball.
- Controlled trapping of the ball.
- Tactical positional play in order to cover as much of the playing field as possible.
- Constant changing of players' own playing position depending on the ball trajectory.
- Timely adopting of the new playing position in order to be able to be as far as possible behind the ball before touching it.
- Lightning fast reaction to opponents' actions.
- Purposeful exploitation of opponents' positioning errors.

Required equipment: four marker cones and one ball per couple.

Rules of the game
- The game starts with an instep kick from the hand.
- The ball must reach at least head height and can bounce only once on the playing field.
- After bouncing, the ball is passed at head height again with one touch by the foot, thigh or head.
- After every mistake (ball out or too low, double touch), the opposing player gets one point and control of the ball.
- The first to get 15 points or whoever is leading after a prearranged time (e.g. 2-5 minutes) wins the game.

This little competition helps the players improve their concentration and feel for the ball.

Variation 1
After it bounces, the ball may be touched as often as desired by the foot, thigh or head before it is kicked up in the air again.

Variation 2
The ball is not allowed to bounce on the ground at all.

Soccer tennis without a net with three players
Three players pass the ball in a predetermined order. The player who cannot pass the ball gets a minus point. If a player gets 5 minus points, he is out.

Soccer tennis without a net – 2v2
The players are numbered from 1-4 before the start, and the ball must always be played in a certain order to ensure that every player is involved.

b) Soccer Circuit

The game 'soccer circuit' is suitable for all ages and abilities, from beginners to pros, thanks to its flexible rules. It doesn't require much space and can be played both indoors and outdoors. Competitions and tournaments can take place on the playing field. However, the basic techniques must be practiced first without scoring.

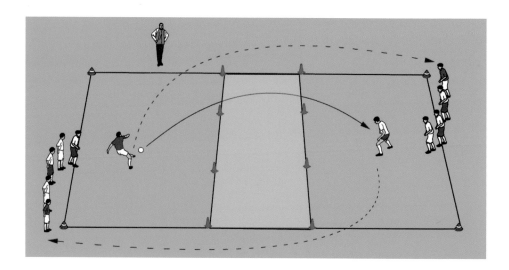

Playing area
- The size of the playing field depends on the age and ability of the players and on the training emphasis. The basic measurement is about 6 x 12 yards.
- There is no net, just a taboo area of 2 x 4 yards that is marked by cones or other training apparatus.

Rules for beginners
- The first player in field A kicks the ball with the instep from the hand over the center area.
- The minimum height is the head height of the players.
- The first player in field B tries to catch the ball. If he succeeds, he kicks the ball to the other half of the playing field. If the ball falls to the ground, he loses a point from his score (2-10 points depending on the target).
- After every high ball, the players change to the other side in a clockwise direction.
- The first to lose all his points loses the game, and the game then starts again.

Coaching tip
The players should have as many points as possible. This ensures that the emphasis is on fun and not on winning!

Variation: let the ball bounce once
The ball must bounce once in the opposite side of the playing field before the player traps it. After the ball bounces, the players pass it once with the foot, thigh or head before trapping it.

Rules for advanced players
The same rules apply as for beginners. The first player in playing field B passes the ball after one bounce to the other side without using his hands.

Beforehand he should 'work' the ball with as many touches as desired. It's advisable to pass the ball as quickly as possible to the other side, though.

And the winner is...
- The first to lose all their points?
- The two players who are left in and win the game? They play off to find the winner, by passing the ball in turn to the other side. Every mistake means one point to the opponent. Who is the first to get two points?
- Who becomes the champion by being the first to win three games?

Rules for 'Pros'

The same rules apply as for beginners and advanced players. The ball should not touch the ground. The players calculate the trajectory of the ball and run quickly to the likely point of impact, where they trap the ball with the foot, thigh or head or pass it directly with the instep or the inside of the foot back into the other side of the playing field.

Variations

- The ball may only be touched twice (when receiving and returning the ball).
- The ball may only be passed after one touch.

And the winner is...

- Each player starts with only one point. One mistake and they're out.
- Which two players are still in and win the game? They play off to decide the winner (see rules for advanced players!). Who becomes the champion by being the first to win three games?

Coaching tip

In this variation, there should be no more than five players per playing field. The coach should therefore set up several playing fields to ensure that as many players are involved as possible.

1.4.2.6   Flicks

Spectacular juggling tricks require an outstanding feel for the ball. The ball must be lifted accurately and deftly and small mistakes be compensated for as fast as lightning.

Flicks are equally difficult to master.

What are Flicks?

Soccer players do not pick up the ball with their hands when they want to juggle. The ball is rolled up, lifted or passed up with a special trick. Lifting the ball in this way is called a flick. The free leg touches the ball first and the other leg is the standing leg.

a) Roll Up

Execution
The ball lies 1-1.5 feet in front of the body, the bottom of the free leg foot drags the ball back onto the instep. Then the ball is lifted and trapped with one or two touches.

Coaching tip
- Depending on the players' ability, it is advisable to first practice dragging the ball back and forth with the sole of the foot as a preliminary drill.
- The roll up can also be done with a change of leg (onto the standing leg).

Errors
- The ball lies too near the standing leg thus preventing adequate contact with the bottom of the foot.
- The ball is rolled up too slowly.
- The ball is lifted too slowly.
- The free leg and standing leg are straightened.

b) Pincer

Execution
The feet are placed shoulder-width apart and the tips of the toes point out diagonally. The ball lies between the feet. The tips of the toes are quickly brought inwards underneath the ball, thus spinning the ball into the air.

Errors
- The feet do not reach the ball at the same time.
- he feet move too slowly.
- The body's center of gravity is too far back.

c) Heel Flick

Execution
In the heel flick, the ball is pushed against the lower leg and is rolled up it with one foot. The ball is then released and passed quickly with the heel to the ground, while moving the foot forward a little. The ball then bounces on the ground and is ready to be juggled.

Coaching tip
If the ball is spun a little, it then bounces slightly forward, thus making it easy to lift it with the instep and juggle with it.

d) Instep Flick

Execution

The instep flick is a variation of the hook flick. The player rolls the ball up the lower leg and pulls it backward slightly. Now he turns his foot so that he touches it with the instep behind the standing leg. This enables the player to spin the ball onto the ground and quickly turn to the high-bouncing ball. He lifts it up with the instep and starts juggling.

e) Maradona Flick

Execution

This is a spectacular way of lifting the ball. The ball lies on the ground in front of the player, who takes a swing with the free leg, (here the right leg), and heels the ball back to the standing leg. At the same time, by moving away the free leg, he lifts the ball with the other (left) foot. This movement should be very fast and dynamic otherwise the ball doesn't gain enough height. The player then starts juggling immediately.

Errors

* Legs too close together or too far apart.
* Too little kicking momentum with the heel.
* Insufficient or wrongly timed swinging movement with the instep.

f) Kick Flick

Execution

The ball lies in front of the player, who takes a swing with the free leg (here the right leg) and moves it toward the ball and goes to kick it. His shooting foot swings past the ball, spinning it slightly and lifting it up. The player catches the falling ball on his instep and starts to juggle.

2   BALL CONTROL

2.1   Basic Theory

The fast pace of the modern game of soccer leaves the player no time to stop the ball, look around and then perform a follow-through action. The players trap the ball on the run and then anticipate another action (dribbling, pass, cross or shot at the goal), and the first touch of the ball is crucial, as with the first touch the player prepares the next move according to the demands of the game situation by:

- retaining possession of the ball and dribbling.
- passing directly or after a second touch to a teammate.
- crossing the ball or shooting directly at the goal.

When waiting to receive a ball, the player must be able to perceive the game situation and what he/she can do with the ball in a split second in order to then be able to take the right tactical decision **before** even receiving the ball.

What must the pass receiver do before receiving the ball?

- Quickly perceive all the important information pertaining to the game situation.
- Make eye contact with the passer and spot free space.
- Run intelligently into an open space (move away from the marking of the opponent, without waiting for the ball, but running towards it) and thus enabling a pass to be made (ideally on the run).

- Use dummy runs in order to deceive the opponent and to be able to trap the ball with as little tackling from the opponent as possible.
- Ensure he/she is balanced just before the first touch of the ball.
- Adopt an open body position that is appropriate for the game situation.
- Find the best follow-through action and disguise your true intentions.

Body position (open, closed)

Closed body position
(body facing the ball, player doesn't see the other players in the direction of play).

Open body position
(looking at ball, body in the direction of play, sees a lot, marks the opponent).

2.2 Practice: Drills Focusing on Ball Control

2.2.1 Ball Control on the Ground

Receiving and running with a low ball with the inside/outside of the foot

Direction of run with the ball
* Diagonally forward.
* About 90° to the left and right.
* Diagonally backward.

Run with the ball diagonally forwards

Set-up
Two cones 5-8 yards apart, one ball, two players

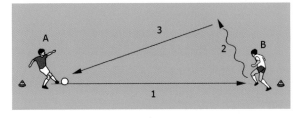

Execution
Player A passes the ball sharply to B, who controls it with the inside of his foot and runs forward with it (to the left or right). After 2-3 yards, he passes the ball back to A and runs back to his cone. Do five reps with the right foot to the left and five with the left foot to the right. Then the players change positions.

Variations
* The players walk/run toward the ball before bringing it under control.
* The players pretend to sprint to the opposite side (dummy run) before bringing the ball under control.
* Bringing the ball under control with the outside of the foot.
* Introduction of an opponent behind the player.

Taking the ball to the side

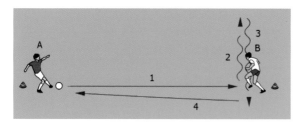

Set-up
Two cones 5-8 yards apart, one ball, two players.

Execution
Player A plays a low ball to B, who controls it with the inside of his foot and runs to the side with it (90° to the left or the right). After 2-3 yards, he passes the ball back to A and runs back to his cone. Five reps with the right foot to the left and five reps with the left foot to the right. The players then change places.

Variations
• The players walk/run toward the ball before running to the side with it.
• The players pretend to sprint to the opposite side before controlling the ball.
• Bringing the ball under control with the outside of the foot.
• Introduction of an opponent behind the player.

One player puts pressure on the player who traps the ball and runs to the side with it.

Taking the ball backwards

Set-up
Two cones 5-8 yards apart, one ball, two players.

Execution
Player A plays a low ball to B, who brings it under control with the inside of the foot and runs backward with it to the left or right. B dribbles around the rear cone to his starting cone and passes the ball back to A. Five reps with the right foot to the left and with the left foot to the right. The players then change places.

Variations
- The players walk/run toward the ball before running backward with it.
- The players pretend to sprint to the opposite side before bringing the ball under control.
- Bringing the ball under control with the outside of the foot.
- Introduction of an opponent behind the player.

Ball control in a square

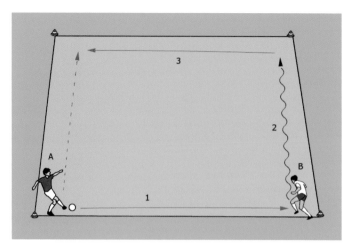

Set-up
Square with sides of 4-6 yards long, one ball, four cones, two players.

Execution
Player A plays a low ball to B, who brings it under control with the inside of his foot and runs with it at a 90° angle toward a free cone. In parallel to this, A also moves to the side, so that he is standing in front of B again. B passes the ball back to A, and so on.

Variations
- Bring the ball under control with the outside of the foot.
- The players run briefly toward the ball before running to the side with it.
- The players start with a dummy run to the side or backward before receiving and running with the ball.

Ball control in groups of three – #1

Set-up
Square with cones 5-8 yards apart, one ball, three players.

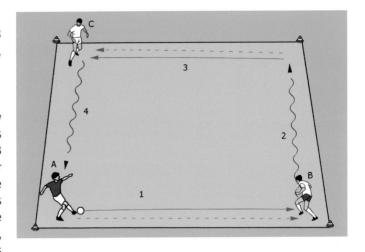

Execution
Player A plays a low ball to B and sprints behind the ball. B brings the ball under control with the inside of his foot and runs with it toward a free cone at a 90° angle, where he then passes to C and sprints behind the ball. C traps the ball, runs with it and passes to A (and so on).

Variations
- Bring the ball under control with the outside of the foot.
- Sprint briefly toward the ball.
- Include dummy runs.

Ball control in groups of three – #2

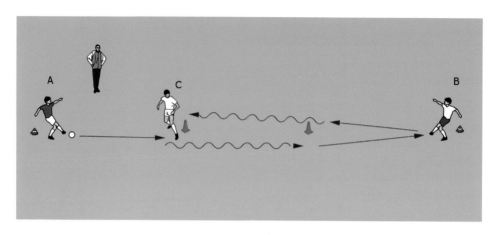

Set-up
Four cones placed in a row 3-5 yards apart, one ball.

Execution
Players A and B stand next to the outside cones. Player C waits at the first center cone for the first pass from A. He brings the ball under control with the inside of his foot and runs with it to the left or right. C dribbles up to the second center cone, where he passes the ball to B, who passes it straight back to him. This action is repeated 10 times, after which the players change places.

Variations
- C runs briefly toward the ball before running backward with it.
- C pretends to sprint to the side before bringing the ball under control.

2.2.2   Controlling Balls in the Air

A surprise high ball behind the defense or a quick change of direction of play causes big problems for any defense.

How can the necessary techniques for this become second nature?

How do players develop the necessary feel for the ball when controlling high balls?

Controlling the ball with the chest

Prepare the body for the follow-through action and run with the ball in the desired direction.

When bringing the ball under control, opponents mark and break away quickly.

Controlling the ball with the thigh

Steeply falling balls are particularly easy to 'defuse' with the thigh. The first touch takes the speed out of the ball and guides it in the desired direction. The player quickly gets into his running rhythm and dribbles off to the side.

Controlling high diagonal balls

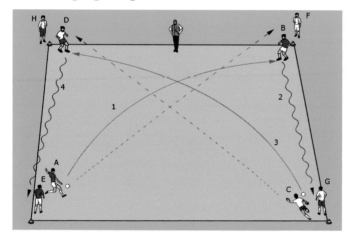

Set-up
Rectangle 16 x 22 yards, four cones, two balls, eight players.

Execution
- A plays a high ball to B and follows the ball. B traps the ball and dribbles toward C.
- C plays a high ball to D and also follows the ball.
- D traps the high ball and dribbles toward E, etc.

Training emphases
- Playing accurate high balls.
- Trapping and running with high balls.

Coaching tips
- Vary the gaps between the cones.
- Introduce opponents at the point of ball reception.

Give and go and diagonal high balls

Set-up
Rectangle 16 x 22 yards, four cones, two balls, 14-18 players.

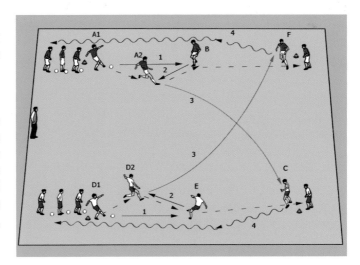

Execution
A plays a give and go with B, who then runs toward F. A plays a high ball to C, who traps the ball and dribbles toward D, the same procedure via D, E and F.

Training emphases
- Give and go.
- Playing accurate high balls.
- Trapping high balls.

Coaching tip
After trapping the ball, quickly get into a space for the next pass to make the drill as fast-moving and effective as possible.

3   DRIBBLING

How can a player successfully shake off an opponent without having learned the necessary tricks? Only players with an extraordinary talent or good observation and cognitive abilities can master the necessary dribbling techniques and feints. All other players are hopelessly out of their depth in a tackle, and all the opponent needs to do is wait until the forward makes a technical error (e.g., ball too far away from the foot). The forwards are inevitably frustrated, while the 'tacklers' emerge victorious. The only way to change this is if the players learn different feints in which they control the ball perfectly. To this end, the Peter Schreiner System© provides a training plan that any coach can immediately put into practice.

3.1   The Peter Schreiner System© (P-S-S)

PSS drills involve the purposeful, effective and methodical teaching of certain basic drills so that they become second nature. The players practice important movements that are always implemented in the same way so intensively and in such a varied way that they are confidently able to recall them in game situations. A wide movement repertoire creates the foundation for creativity and decision-making ability. Only once a player has mastered different feints with the left and right feet and alternative follow-through actions is he in a position to outwit and outplay an opponent in a 1 on 1 situation, or even a complete defense.

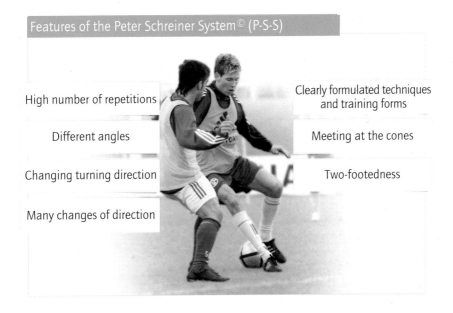

Features of the Peter Schreiner System© (P-S-S)

High number of repetitions

Different angles

Changing turning direction

Many changes of direction

Clearly formulated techniques and training forms

Meeting at the cones

Two-footedness

3.2   Features of the Peter Schreiner System[©]

High number of repetitions of motivating drills

A coach should have a large treasury of different drills at his disposal and constantly expose his players to new learning situations. In the PSS, players learn basic movements (dribbling, feints) and repeat them in a variety of drills until they master them perfectly.

In tennis, pros practice even simple shots over and over again so that they make as few mistakes as possible in tournaments when they are highly stressed.

Meeting at the cones

Before the players dribble in the PSS for the first time, the coach should tell the players that basically they just move slightly to the side of the cones and don't dribble around them, thus remaining the same distance away from them as they would be from an opponent. The change of direction **before** the cones forces the players to raise their heads and to make sure that they don't bump into the players on the other side of the cones. In addition, this conveys the feeling of practicing in a group even when the player is performing a solo drill.

Many changes of direction

In the PSS, players change direction many times. They learn to control their bodies and the ball in such a way that they are able to move with the ball in any direction they want. The players improve their feel for the ball, they master the ball, perceive their opponent's position and turn away to the correct side, thereby skillfully shielding the ball.

Different angles

The change of drills and the change in distances between the markers produce different angles, so that every angle constitutes a new challenge for the player. Kicking with the inside of the foot is completely different for a 90° turn than for a 180° turn, as in the 'Comb' for example.

Two-footedness

The technical tasks force the players to practice with both feet. For example, if a player is kicking with the inside of the foot at the cones, he must change feet at each cone otherwise the drill cannot be completed. Particularly in basic training, players should learn to dribble with both feet and to feint to both sides.

Turning direction: left and right

Young players in particular may find that they become disoriented after turning around their body's longitudinal axis and then dribble to the wrong cone. This is why special emphasis is placed on turning around this axis in the methodical sequence of basic movements. It is advisable first to practice the turns without a ball or with the ball in your hand before kicking the ball with the feet.

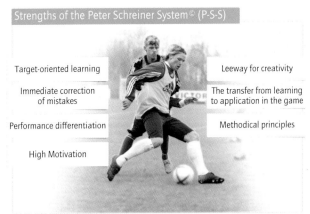

Strengths of the Peter Schreiner System© (P-S-S)

Target-oriented learning

Immediate correction of mistakes

Performance differentiation

High Motivation

Leeway for creativity

The transfer from learning to application in the game

Methodical principles

Strengths of the
Peter Schreiner System©

3.3 Strengths of the Peter Schreiner System©

Immediate correction of mistakes

All players are part of a system and complete the set activities. Beginners dribble through the set-ups slowly and with concentration, while advanced players do it quickly. The coach can easily see all the players and can talk to each player directly, so that specific mistakes can be corrected immediately. An advantage of the large group drills is that the coach can give an individual correction while the other players keep on practicing and don't stand around waiting. However, he should discuss common mistakes in front of the whole group.

Target-oriented learning

The activities and technical tasks are clearly formulated. The coach observes the players and the PSS enables him/her to start a purposeful learning process. As the players all use the same technique in a learning phase, the coach sees immediately whether they have accomplished the training goal. If a player needs more practice to learn a technique, the coach should set additional drills as homework.

Performance differentiation

Girls and boys, beginners and advanced players can train together in the PSS. The difference between them lies in the speed of execution, the degree of difficulty of the techniques or in the variable use of different techniques.

At the starting cone, the coach sets a strong player a more difficult task than a weaker one. The coach can also control the conditioning load. While the first group practices different techniques slowly, a group with advanced players gets the special task of performing basic tasks so fast that they complete two circuits in the same time that the beginners' group complete one.

Methodical principles

The drills and the choice of feints are determined by the fitness and ability of the players. The coach describes new movements to his/her players and allows them to perform them slowly and technically correctly before they become second nature by dint of constant practice. The difficulty of the movement involved, the complexity of the set-up, the pace of execution (time pressure) and the introduction of an opponent (opponent pressure) should continually be increased.

Leeway for creativity

As well as set tasks, effective dribbling training should always also leave leeway for the players' own ideas and creative application of the learned techniques. A spectacular trick that a player spontaneously performs is just as important for the learning process as a feint from the training program. The coach should always have time to praise a player and offer him the opportunity to perform his trick. It is often amazing to see how imaginative and creative players can be.

High Motivation

Experiences in clubs, schools and soccer academies have shown that players enjoy practicing basic skills. The PSS guarantees high player motivation. This is further reinforced if the players notice that they are gaining confidence with the ball and mastering techniques that are attractive and spectacular. The change of drills and techniques ensure that training is never boring. The players should under no circumstances be allowed to get fed up with the PSS, though.

The transfer from learning to application

After the basic training, the players should first use the learned feints that are now second nature in straightforward set game situations, then in training games and lastly in competitive matches. Dribbling training is only successful if the learned techniques can also be reproduced in a match.

3.4   Basic Theory

3.4.1   Ball Control, Ball Driving, Dribbling and Feints

Guiding the ball

A slow and controlled forward movement with a ball that stays close to the player's foot is called **guiding the ball**. Guiding the ball can aid reorientation in the space, i.e. finding teammates or giving a teammate the possibility to run into a free space. The player should not be looking at the ball to allow him/her to see what is going on in the game.

Driving the ball (tempo dribbling)

Driving the ball or **tempo dribbling** is used to cover free space as quickly as possible. The ball does not stay as close to the foot as in ball control, but should always be under control. If the situation requires, the player should be able to change the direction or the pace, or to interrupt the forward movement.

Dribbling

Dribbling means 'to move forward with small kicks.' In a narrower sense, dribbling requires the proximity of an opponent, who the dribbler would like to defeat. Dribbling is often preceded by one or more feints.

Feints

Feints are based on the principle of false information. When feinting, the dribbler disguises his true intention by an 'apparent movement' (change of speed or direction, body movement, etc.) and then carries out his plan. The opponent should be caused to react wrongly, thus giving the attacker a small time advantage. In a feint, a skilled dribbler exploits the opponent's reactions and seems very convincing in the execution of his feint.

3.4.2   A Good Dribbler Should...

- possess good body control and balance.
- be able to observe attentively and interpret the reactions of the defender (anticipation of the opponent's intentions).
- possess a good feel for the ball.
- master dribbling techniques and feints with variations (technical playing qualities of a dribbler).
- good timing in the use of feints (time aspect of a feint).
- possess excellent orientation (spatial aspect of a feint).

These qualities enable the player to spot gaps and give him the technique with which to dribble through two players.

3.4.3   10 Basic Rules for a Good Dribbler

1. Dribbling in the vicinity of an opponent should be preceded by a situation-appropriate **feint**, which causes the opponent to react in the wrong way, thereby creating a slight time advantage.

2. After the feint, the attacker should continue dribbling **as explosively as possible**, so that the time advantage is not lost.

3. The dribbler's **center of gravity** should be low so that he is balanced and can start to run in any direction.

4. A skilled dribbler decoys his opponent out of his waiting position so that he does not dribble up to him head on but to the side of him, in order to disturb his **stable posture**. If the defender reacts to the movement, it is likely to cause him to adopt an unfavorable body position which makes it hard for him to react quickly. A feint with sudden change of direction is particularly effective if the opponent has to slow down a movement in order to move in another direction.

5. A skillful dribbler considers his **own strengths** when performing a feint. There are feints which are particularly suited to fast attacking players (e.g., on the wing with space gained after the feint) and those that are preferred by nimble players who are good ball handlers (e.g., in the penalty box).

6. The dribbler should observe the **opponent's behavior** closely in order to be able to react appropriately to the defender's reactions. If a feint does not accomplish the desired effect, then further action is required. A second feint could further destabilize the defender and eventually put him on the wrong foot. At the start of a game, an attacker should quickly spot the defenders' qualities (e.g., reaction and action speed) and take them into account in his feints.

7. A feint should not be carried out **too soon** or **too far away**, for this gives the opponent time to compensate for his mistake. However, if the feint is performed **too late** or **too close** to the dribbler, the attacker is likely to lose the ball. With match experience, a dribbler acquires a feel for the right distance to the opponent.

8. Dribbling should always be necessary and **never done for the sake of it**, but always serve the interests of the team. A player, for whom performing a 'nutmeg' or embarrassing an opponent are more important than a smart pass to a teammate, weakens his/her team, for he/she slows down the attack. As well as technique, the player must also learn when dribbling is necessary or if a pass would be more appropriate.

9. Dribbling should not represent a **direct danger of an own goal**. A player should therefore avoid dribbling in his own penalty box or without defensive back-up.

10. One should only use feints in matches that one has practiced many times and therefore **confidently masters**. A badly executed feint destabilizes the dribbler and reduced his self-confidence.

3.4.4 Dribbling Is only Useful or Necessary When...

- an attacker has nobody to pass to.
- a defender must be moved out of the way for tactical reasons.
- a shot at goal should be prepared.
- it is necessary to play for time.
- a breakthrough into free space is started.
- a 1v1 situation near the goal must be won.
- there is a need to open up room to move.
- time must be given to teammates to catch up.
- an offside trap should be avoided.

3.4.5 Learning to Dribble in the Peter Schreiner System©

Learning process of sports movements

The teaching of sports movements should not be haphazard, as is unfortunately still often the case with our up and coming soccer talent. Many coaches have no long-term training plan, but plan their training from week to week or from training session to training session. Even the choice of training content tends to be rather haphazard. Many coaches feel that organizing systematically planned and methodologically sound training that is suitable for children is too difficult. The PSS provides the coach with a syllabus for teaching dribbling, feints and a feel for the ball.

Technical demonstrations

A demonstration should be technically perfect. It is therefore better to ask a technically accomplished player to demonstrate a difficult basic movement than to demonstrate an incorrect movement oneself. It is often enough though just to describe a new movement slowly for the players to understand the basic pattern. Talented players will usually quickly understand which technique is required and can then demonstrate it to the other players.

Repetition with observation focuses

Particularly difficult movements should be repeated many times, for which the coach sets different specific observation tasks that show that the players have also really understood the important partial movements.

Detailed demonstration (individual parts of the body or in slow motion)

It is sometimes advisable to draw attention to individual parts of the body in detail. Important phases can also be performed in slow motion so that the players see and understand.

The correction of mistakes

The coach supports and guides the learning process by a targeted correction of mistakes taking the following points into account.

- Information is better given in short bursts than in long explanations.
- Always correct mistakes one at a time; never several mistakes at the same time.
- Don't get bogged down in details, which could confuse or turn off players, but emphasize the main points.
- Give frequent positive reinforcement (praise and encouragement).
- Discuss mistakes when all players have performed the drill and are ready to listen.
- Individual corrections while an drill is being performed should be short and detail-specific.

- Do not correct mistakes immediately, but give players the chance to see their own mistakes for themselves. This can be done by making the players aware of their mistakes by means of clever questioning.

Here is a tried and tested sequence for learning feints.

- Provide a clear presentation of the movement by using photos, videos or demonstration by a player.
- Try out and practice new moves slowly without an opponent.
- Automate the movement in different drills.
- A passive (partially active) opponent provides orientation (spatial and chronological) and a connection to the game situation. (The correct choice of distance from the opponent, and the correct timing of a feint require practice and experience).
- Use mastered feints in mini matches, in realistic game situations and in matches. (It is advisable to practice feints in their typical game situations right from the start and point out possible applications. The purpose of the feint should always be clear to the player).
- The principle objective should be the use of the learned technique in a competitive game. (Only under the pressure of an opponent in match conditions can the dribbler show that he has truly mastered a trick).

3.5   Practice: Dribbling and Feint Training

3.5.1 Basic Drills in Small Groups

The difference between the drills for small groups (pairs, groups of three or four) lies in the position of the attacking opponent. The game situation 'attacker deceives defender and dribbles around him' requires other drills depending on whether the opponent is situated **directly in front** of, **behind** or **to the side of** the attacker.

3.5.1.1 Opponent in Front

There are different ways of deceiving an opponent who is situated in front of the attacker.

Here are a few examples:

a) Dummy Step

Lunge to the left with the left leg and take the ball past the opponent with the outside of the right foot.

b) Rivelino Trick

With the right foot, take a step around the ball to the left and take the ball with the outside of the right foot and outplay the opponent.

c) Drag-back with the Sole of the Foot

Away from the standing leg
Drag the ball back with the sole of the right foot, immediately pull the ball to the side with the inside of the right foot and dribble away from the opponent.

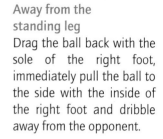

Across the standing leg
Pull the ball back with the sole of the left foot, immediately pull the ball to the side with the inside of the left foot across the standing leg and dribble past the opponent.

Drag-back with the sole of the foot behind the standing leg
Drag the ball back with the sole of the left foot, immediately pull the ball to the side with the inside of the left foot behind the standing leg and dribble past the opponent.

d) 270-degree turn with the inside of the foot

Shield the ball with the body by turning left around the ball, while pulling the ball twice around with the inside of the right foot, and dribble away from the opponent immediately after the turn.

Variation
Perform the same turn with the outside of the foot, as frequently demonstrated by Franz Beckenbauer.

e) Matthews Trick

Drag the ball back slightly to the left with the inside of the right foot and pretend to break away to the left side, lift the ball with the outside of the right foot (the outer instep) over the attacking foot of the opponent and dribble past the opponent down the right side.

3.5.1.2   Drills – Opponent in Front

a) Opponent in Front in Pairs

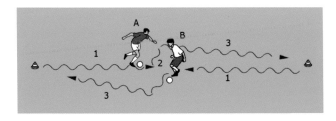

Set-up
The players pair up and each pair is given a ball and a starting cone.
Distance 5-7 yards.

Execution
Two players dribble between two cones toward each other and dodge each other in a predetermined way (e.g., with a dummy step). When they reach the cones they turn around and repeat the drill.

Variations
- dummy step/step-over/scissors.
- drag-back with the sole of the foot.
- Matthews Trick.
- 270-degree turn inwards.

Coaching tip
It is important that the players agree beforehand to which side they are going to dodge, although the basic movements should be performed to both sides.

b) Opponent in Front in Groups of Four

Set-up
Pairs of players each stand next to a cone with a ball.
Distance: 8-10 yards.

Execution
A and B dribble toward each other, perform a feint in the middle at the same time and dribble past each other. A passes to C and B to D, who trap the ball and also dribble toward each other.

Variations
• dummy step/step-over/cissors.
• drag-back with the sole of the foot and inside of the foot.
• Matthews Trick.
• 270-degree turn inwards.

c) Opponent in Front in groups of Six

Set-up
One player at each corner of a triangle and one player in the center without a ball (length of sides: 6-10 yards).

Execution
Three dribblers start at the same time from the corners of the triangle. In the middle of the sides of the triangle stand the opponents, who must be dribbled around to the outside or the inside. After a prearranged time, players swap tasks. The dribblers go into the center and the defenders become dribblers.

Variations
- dummy step/step-over/scissors.
- drag-back with the sole of the foot and inside of the foot.
- Matthews Trick.
- perform the drill in a square (group of eight).

Coaching tips
- The resistance of the defenders should constantly be increased.
- The coach or a player gives the starting signal.

d) Triangle with Center

Set-up
Triangle with center, distance to the middle 5-7 yards. A player stands at each corner with a ball.

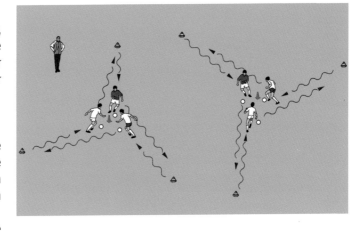

Execution
Three players dribble at the same time toward the center of a triangle and meet in the middle. About 1 yard before the cone they perform a feint (opponent in front) and dribble toward the next cone. They wait until all players have reached their cone and after a brief eye contact or starting signal of a leader they start playing again in a clockwise direction.

Variation
After a certain number of circuits, they change direction in order to train both feet.

e) Square with Center

Set-up
Square with center, distance to the middle 5-7 yards. A player stands at each corner with a ball

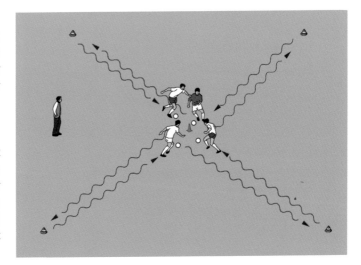

Execution
Four players start dribbling at the same time toward the center of a square, perform a feint (opponent in front) and dribble to the next cone in the square.

3.5.1.3 Opponent to the Side

This sections features techniques and drills which involve players performing a high number of repetitions of the basic movements required when an opponent attacks from the side.

Let's start with a few examples for possible basic movements.

a) 270-degree Turn Inward

b) 270-degree Turn Outward

c) Drag-back with the Sole of the Foot

3.5.1.4   Drills – Opponent from the Side

a) Circle with center

Set-up
Circle with center, distance to the center 5-7 yards. A player with a ball stands at each cone.

Execution
5-8 players dribble into the center of a circle and turn about 1 yard before the center cone back to their cone. This requires a 180° turn.

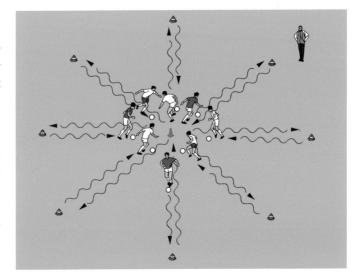

Possible techniques
- Drag the ball back with the sole of the foot.
- Kick with the inside/outside of the foot.
- Scissors inside-inside.
- Drag the ball behind the standing leg.

b) Attacks in a triangle

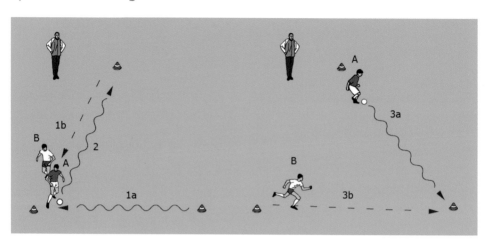

Set-up
Partner drill with a ball in a triangle.

Execution
One player dribbles in a clockwise direction from corner to corner in the triangle, while another player attacks in the opposite direction. The dribbler shields the ball and dribbles to the next cone.

Possible techniques
• kicking the ball with the inside of the foot.
• kicking the ball with the outside of the foot.
• 270-degree turn inward.
• 270-degree turn outward.
• drag-back with the sole of the foot.

Variation
• The dribbler moves counterclockwise.

Coaching tip
The players learn to shield the ball from, and then quickly dribble away from, an opponent who attacks from the side.

c) Attack from the side

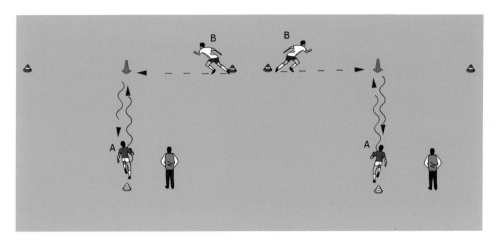

Set-up
Four cones form a T shape. An attacker dribbles to the center cone; a defender attacks from the left or right side.

Execution
A dribbles up to the center cone. The defender B attacks from the right. A turns 180° away from B and dribbles back to the starting cone. The defender runs between both cones forward and backward so that the same drill situation is constantly recreated. After a prearranged time or number of reps, the players change roles.

Variations
• The defender attacks from the left then the dribbler performs a 180° turn to the right.
• The defender runs straight to the opposite cone so that the dribbler must constantly turn in different directions, first to the left, then to the right.

Coaching tip
The defender should sprint convincingly toward the ball and simulate an attack.

3.5.2   Large Group Training

3.5.2.1   Basic Theory

Years ago, I often used a Wiel Coerver drill, which involves 16 children dribbling according to a certain system around a cone circuit, after starting at four different points. It was a **zigzag shape**. At the time I called this drill 'large group training,' because it can accommodate an almost unlimited number of players. The more children taking part, the more cones are used so that the players don't have to wait too long at the start. The possibilities of the zigzag are however limited as the angle is always the same.

I wondered, what about the forward and backward movement, what about the **180° turn**?

At a basic training session at FC Schalke 04 in Germany, I had the idea of placing the cones differently so that this 180° turn was often solicited.

I called this new drill 'Comb' because in my diagrams it looked a bit like a comb. In this shape, special techniques are trained that are necessary in many game situations. The 'scissors' or the 'pulling under the standing leg.' After further experiments with new shapes, new angles and new endless drills, I came up with the **Christmas Tree**, the **Thunderbolt** and the **Figure eight dribble**.

Large group drills are suitable for...
* ...warming up.
* ...learning and automatizing basic movements (dribbling with the right and left foot, changing direction and turning with the ball, special foot and leg movements, feints for different game situations).
* ....motivating running training.

Warm-up or main training?
The large group drills are just as valuable in the warm-up as in the main part of a workout. While in the warm-up, familiar movements can be carried out at a moderate pace, during the workout the coach introduces new movements or has his players perform basic movements at match pace.

Coaching tips
Every new large group drill initially represents a challenge to the players' orientation. They should first understand the path they must take through the cones before practicing special techniques. That is why the players first run through the dribbling circuit with the ball in their hand or without a ball, thus ensuring that they can concentrate on the circuit. The coach should not spend a long time explaining and describing, but demonstrate the path by running it himself.

Then the players dribble freely and without technique guidelines with the ball. Strong players experiment and show the coach different techniques.

Beginners use a simple technique and are content if they manage to dribble along the path. If the players confidently master the path, they then practice specific different techniques.

There follow a presentation of special tasks, techniques, technique combinations and creative applications.

3.5.2.2 Zigzag

The zigzag is a very quick and simple way of automatizing important basic movements and a very effective dribbling workout can be organized with just a few cones. Just changing the layout of the cones offers many variants with different angles and distances. The distances between the cones depend on the abilities and training goals of the players.

Preliminary drill: Zigzag with a partner

Set-up
A and B stand with a ball at the starting cone. A diamond shape is laid out in front of them.

Execution
A dribbles from cone to cone with different movements and changes of direction. At the last cone, he passes the ball to B (2), who starts the next lap.

Possible techniques
- kick with the inside/outside of the foot.
- 270-degree turn inward/outward.
- drag-back with the sole of the foot.

Variations
- clockwise.
- counterclockwise.

Zigzag with follow-through action in groups of three

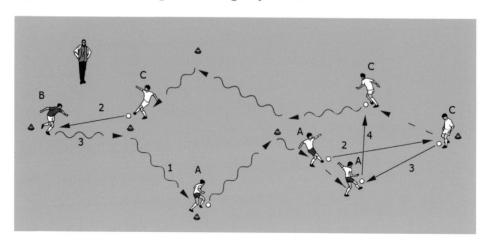

Set-up
A diamond shape is laid out between two end cones. A and B stand at the starting cone with a ball. C waits at the opposite end.

Execution
A dribbles from the starting cone through the diamond to C on the other side, where both play a give and go. A takes over C's position, C dribbles toward B at the starting cone, where C passes the ball to B, etc.

Possible techniques in der Raute
- kick with the inside of the foot.
- kick with the outside of the foot.
- 270-degree turn inwards.
- 270-degree turn outwards.
- drag-back with the sole of the foot – instep.

Variations
- clockwise.
- counterclockwise.
- give and go at both ends.
- attack at the start.

Double Zigzag

Set-up
Seven cones are laid out in a zigzag shape 1-2-1-2-1, which are dribbled through in an infinite loop.

Execution
The Double Zigzag has a start and finish. With seven cones, eight players can easily train purposefully in the Double Zigzag. The zigzag can also be extended, so that the players have to negotiate several cones before they reach the turning marker. The distance and angles between the cones can also be varied.

Possible techniques
- kick with the inside/outside of the foot.
- 270-degree turn inwards/outwards.
- dummy step/step-over/scissors.
- drag back with the sole of the foot.

Quadruple Zigzag

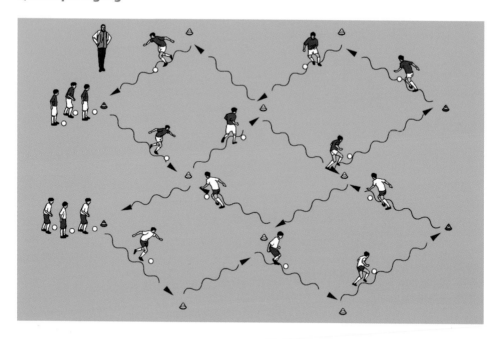

Set-up

12 cones are laid out in a zigzag shape, through which the players dribble in an infinite loop. Set-up of the cones: 2-3-2-3-2

Execution

The most important drill for team training is the Quadruple Zigzag. There are two starts and two turning points. The dribblers meet each other at several points within this layout and are therefore forced to take their eye off the ball and observe the other dribblers. The players dribble and turn with the ball to the left and to the right.

Possible techniques
- kick with the inside of the foot/outside of the foot.
- 70 degree turn inwards/outwards.
- dummy step/step-over/scissors.
- drag back with the sole of the foot.

Variations
- start to the right.
- start to the left.
- three or four starting and turning cones.

Below is a tried and tested system for the Zigzag

- **Run through – holding the ball:** the players first run through the drill in order to familiarize themselves with the path.

- **Run through – kicking the ball:** in the second step they dribble the ball through the circuit with a technique of their choice.

- **Kicking with the inside of the foot:** the simplest change of direction in the zigzag is with the inside of the foot. Experience has shown that beginners are quick to learn this technique.

- **Kicking with the outside of the foot:** After the inside of the foot, players learn to kick with the outside of the foot, with both feet.

- **Kicking with the inside and outside of the foot alternately:** just as difficult is the change from inside to outside, i.e. kicking with just one foot. Children start with their stronger foot but must also practice with their weaker foot.

- **Dummy step/step-over/scissors:** once the players master kicking with the outside of the foot, the next stage is the dummy step. Progressing to the step-over and the scissors is then no great obstacle, for the only difference is in the foot and leg action. In the dummy step, the foot bypasses the ball, in the step-over, over the ball and in the scissors, around the ball.

- **270-degree turn inwards:** One of the most important basic movements in basic training is the 270-degree turn with the inside of the foot. This turn is a double change of direction against the dribbling direction. If the player wants to pull out to the left, he turns his body around to the right.

- **270-degree turn outwards:** Advanced players like this turn, but it can present problems for beginners. This was a speciality of Beckenbauer, who liked to follow it with a volley with the outside of the foot.

- **Drag-back with the sole of the foot:** this trick can be successfully automated in the zigzag. The dribbler pulls the ball back with the sole of the foot and dribbles to the next cone. The second touch (dribbling in the new direction) is possible with the inside of the foot or with the instep.

- **Drag behind the standing leg:** the most difficult technique of basic training in the zigzag is the 'drag behind the standing leg.' Here, the other foot drags the ball back and guides it behind the standing leg to the next cone. So, if the player wants to dodge to the left, he drags the ball back with the right foot and then past the standing leg to the left.

- **Combination of different techniques:** if all these techniques are practiced, the coach can use different combinations, e.g. the change from 'kicking with the inside of the foot' and '270-degree turn inwards' or the combination of 'dummy' and 'drag back with the sole of the foot.' The players should then freely and independently combine different techniques.

3.5.2.3 The Christmas Tree

Creative dribblers have a huge repertoire of feints and alternative moves. Already in basic training, players should learn several moves of different types and automatate them in different drills. The Christmas Tree has other angles and therefore offers new possibilities for performing turns and changes of direction with techniques that are different to the zigzag.

Basic Elements of the Christmas Tree

The Christmas Tree, like the zigzag, creates the framework for a motivating dribbling drill. All players are constantly moving, have a great deal of ball contact and systematically practice new moves. This enables them to improve their feel for the ball very economically and effectively. With this second drill, the coach can allow the varied practice of basic movements. He can easily see all the players, can motivate and correct and therefore purposefully implement learning processes. With six cones (2-3-1), the basic elements can be built up in which 2-3 players can practice.

Preliminary Drill Christmas Tree with Partner

Set-up
A and B stand with a ball at the starting cone. In front of them, cones are set out in the shape of a Christmas tree.

Execution
A dribbles with different moves and changes of direction through the course. At the last cone he passes the ball to B (2), who starts the next circuit.

Technique Combinations
* kicking with the inside of the foot x 2.
* 270-degree turn inwards, then outwards.
* dummy step/step-over/scissors.
* Drag back behind the standing leg.
* drag the ball back with the sole of the foot.

Variations
* clockwise.
* counterclockwise.

Christmas Tree in groups of three

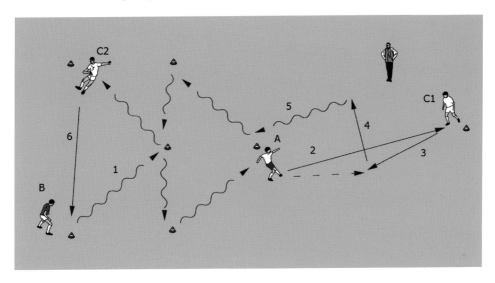

Set-up
At the starting cone of a circuit in the shape of a Christmas Tree stand A and B with a ball. C waits for them on the opposite side.

Execution
A dribbles from the starting cone through the Christmas Tree to C on the other side, where they both play a give and go. A takes C's place and C dribbles to B at the starting cone where C passes the ball to B, etc.

Variations
- introduction of two balls (quicker execution).
- clockwise.
- counterclockwise.

Christmas Tree in pairs

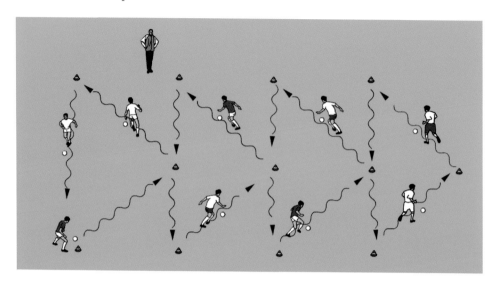

Set-up
The cones are set out as for the Christmas Tree: 2-3-3-3-1. The dribbling directions are: diagonal to the center, then outwards. The distance between the two starting cones is approx. 6-10 yards. The distance between other cones is dependent on the age of the players.

Execution
The players start at the right cone and dribble diagonally to the center, then outwards, diagonally to the center, then outwards, etc., until they reach the last cone, the top of the Christmas Tree. The dribbling speed should get faster and faster.

Techniques
Kicking with the inside/outside of the foot, 270-degree turn inwards/outwards, dummy step/step-over/scissors, drag back behind the standing leg, drag back with the sole of the foot.

Coaching tips
- The Christmas Tree, like the Zigzag, creates the framework for a motivating dribbling drill. It allows the coach to observe and manage the players.
- All players are constantly on the go, have a great deal of contact with the ball and systematically practice new moves, thereby very effectively improving their feel for the ball.
- The coach can see all players easily, can motivate and correct, thereby implementing learning processes.

Christmas Tree for 4 players

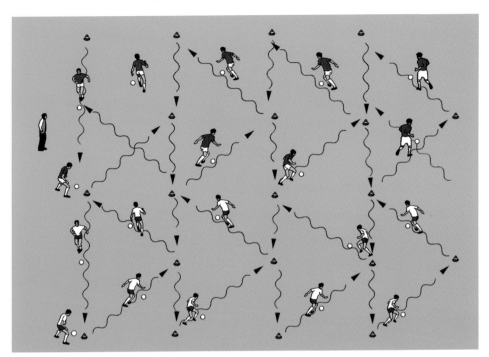

Set-up
Lay out two Christmas Trees side by side: 3-5-5-5-2. The dribbling directions are again: diagonal to the center, then outwards. The starting cones are 6-10 yards apart.

Execution
The Christmas Tree for 4 players is intended for large groups and for a whole team. The advantage is that the players meet very frequently at the center cones. They must take their eyes off the ball so that they don't get in the way of the players on the other side of the cones. Depending on the technique task, they dribble with the left or right foot and turn to the left or right around the cones.

Techniques
Kicking with the inside/outside of the foot, 270 degree turn inwards/outwards, dummy step/step-over/scissors, drag back behind the standing leg, drag back with the sole of the foot.

Variation
Start to the right or to the left.

3.5.2.4   Thunderbolt

In order to be able to practice the game situation 'opponent head-on' in a row, it is necessary to run to the side (left or right) from dribbling straight ahead. In the Thunderbolt, the players practice the 'Matthews Trick' or the 'scissors' very intensively when dribbling straight ahead.

At the outside cones, the players repeat the technique of the fir tree drill, at the center cones, techniques are required at a 90° angle, so that the different drills complement each other. Repetitions consolidate what has been learned previously.

Preliminary Thunderbolt with a partner

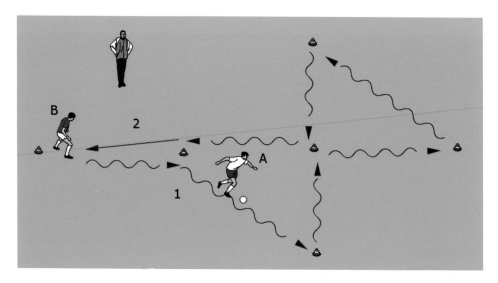

Set-up
The cones are laid out as in the diagram (diamond with a center), two players stand at the start with one ball.

Execution
The first player A dribbles through the course (forward, diagonally outwards, to the center, forward). At the last cones of the whole circuit, he passes the ball to B.

Variations
- clockwise.
- counterclockwise.

Thunderbolt in groups of three

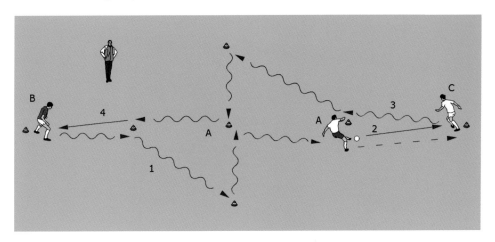

Set-up
The 'Thunderbolt' circuit is extended by placing a cone at the end, where C waits for a pass from dribbler A.

Execution
A dribbles (1) from the starting cone through the Thunderbolt and at the end plays a give and go with C (2, 3), who takes the ball and dribbles back through the course with it. At the end cone, B receives the ball (4) and likewise dribbles through the course then plays a give and go with A.

Tips and hints
- Quick and accurate passing game at the end of the course.
- Use a variety of techniques when dribbling and when changing direction.

Variations
- clockwise.
- counterclockwise.
- give and go at both ends.

Double Thunderbolt

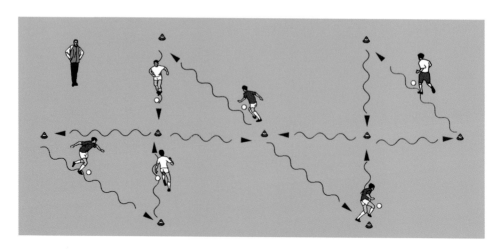

Set-up

The cones are laid out in a 1-3-1-3-1 system, and the dribbling directions in the Thunderbolt are: diagonally outwards – diagonally to the center – forward – diagonally to the side – etc.

Execution

The Thunderbolt with a starting and turning point is called the 'Double Thunderbolt.' Up to eight players practice at the same time. The actual training focus lies at the center cone. The dummy step, the step-over, the scissors, the Matthews Trick or the drag back with the sole of the foot after a dummy shot are very good ways of practicing outplaying an opponent who is approaching head-on.

Coaching tip
- Introduction of an opponent who establishes the orientation to the game situation.

Variations
- clockwise.
- counterclockwise.

Quadruple Thunderbolt

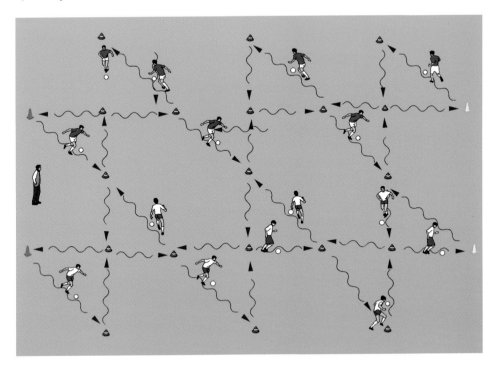

Set-up
The cones are laid out in a 2-5-2-5-2-5-2 system, each player has a ball.

Execution
The Quadruple Thunderbolt has two starting and turning points and is suitable for a whole team. Depending on the number of players, the coach can place three or four Thunderbolts one behind the other. There should be no waiting at the starting cone.

Techniques
Kick with the inside/outside of the foot, 270-degree turn inwards/outwards, dummy step/step-over/scissors, drag back behind the standing leg, drag back with the sole of the foot.

Variations
- start to the right.
- start to the left.

3.5.2.5 Comb

The training focus in the 'Comb' drill is the forward and backward movement (180° changes of direction). The dribbling directions, which the coach should always determine beforehand, are: forwards – to the center – back, etc.

At the end of the first row, the players dribble over to the other side and start going back to the start with the same dribbling directions: forwards – to the center – back – forwards.

Two different turns are therefore solicited (90° and 180°).

Preliminary drill: Comb with a Partner

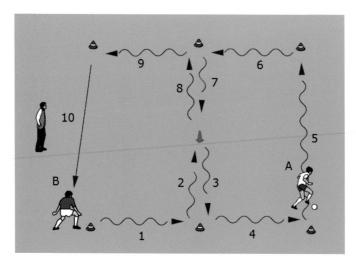

Set-up
A and B stand with a ball at the starting cone of the course 2-3-2.

Execution
A dribbles forward – to the center – back, forwards – to the other side, then back to the end cone. There he passes the ball to B, who takes it and dribbles through the course with it.

Coaching tip
In this basic form, the players particularly practice the 180° turn techniques at the center cone.

Techniques
• Drag the ball back with the sole of the foot.
• Kick with the inside of the foot.
• Kick with the outside of the foot.
• Scissors.
• Drag back behind the standing leg.

Variations
• clockwise.
• counterclockwise.

Comb with follow-through action in groups of three

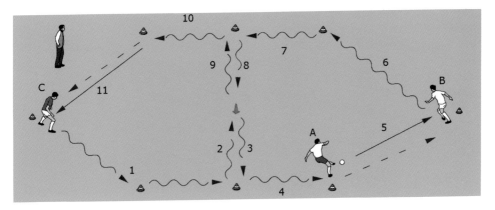

Set-up
A and B stand with a ball at the starting cone of the course 1-2-3-2-1.

Execution
A dribbles to the right to the first cone, then forward – to the center – forwards (1-4). At the last cone, he passes to B (5), who takes the ball and dribbles through the course (6-10). At the last cone, B passes to C (11), who completes the circuit.

Coaching tip
This basic form allows the players to practice the 180° turn techniques, particularly at the center cone.

Techniques
Drag back with the sole of the foot, kick with the inside/outside of the foot, scissors, drag back behind the standing leg.

Variations
• start to the right.
• start to the left.

180° Dribbling in the 'Comb'

Double Comb

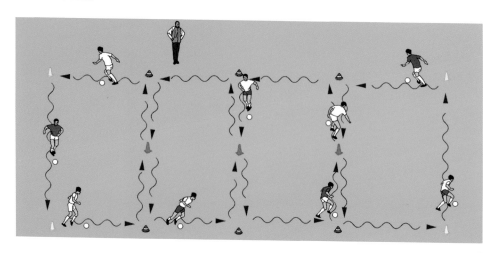

Set-up
Layout of the course: 2-3-3-3-2, each player has a ball.

Execution
The double comb with 13 cones allows up to eight players to practice. The second player starts when the first player dribbles forward in the next lane. The distance between the cones can be easily adapted to all ages and abilities. The dribbling speed should gradually increase.

90° turn techniques
- kick with the inside of the foot.
- kick with the outside of the foot.
- 270-degree turn inwards/outwards.
- dummy step/step-over/scissors.
- drag the ball back with the sole of the foot.

180° turn techniques

- drag the ball back with the sole of the foot.
- kick with the inside of the foot.
- kick with the outside of the foot.
- scissors.
- drag back behind the standing leg.

Quadruple Comb

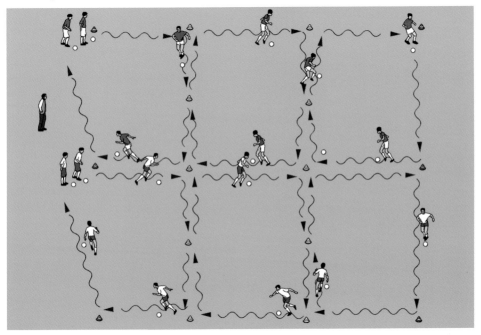

Set-up

Layout of the course: 3-5-5-3, each player has a ball.

Execution

The Quadruple Comb is the most important drill for team training. It has two starting and two turning points. The second player starts when the first dribbles forward in the next lane. The players stay on their sides and dribble past the players in the other groups.

Variations

- clockwise.
- counterclockwise.

3.5.2.6 Figure Eight Dribbling

Figure Eight Dribbling takes place around a square with the following prearranged dribbling directions: diagonally forward (to the left) – back – diagonally forward (to the right).

The turns can all be performed both to the right and to the left, thus changing the type and difficulty of the basic techniques at the cones.

For example, if after the first diagonal path, the player turns left with the inside of the right foot at the cone, that involves changing direction with the inside of the foot. However, if he turns to the right, then he performs a 270-degree turn inwards.

Preliminary drill: Figure Eight Dribbling with a partner

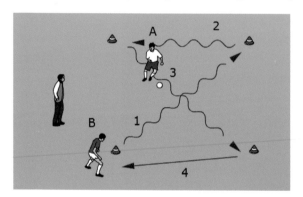

Set-up
At the starting cone of a square, two players stand with a ball.

Execution
A dribbles diagonally forward – back – diagonally forward and then passes to B, who likewise dribbles in a figure eight through the square.

Figure Eight Dribbling techniques
- kick with the inside/outside of the foot.
- 270-degree turn inwards/outwards.
- drag the ball back with the sole of the foot.
- pull the ball back behind the standing leg – with right and left legs.
- dummy step/step-over/scissors.

Variation
start to the right/to the left.

Figure Eight Dribbling in groups of three

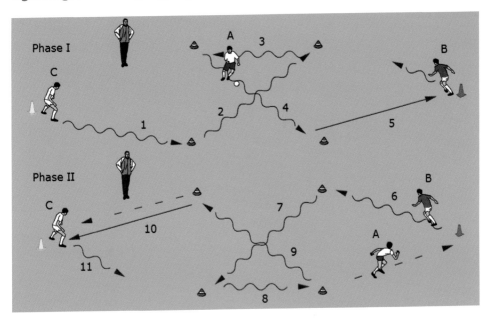

Set-up
The course consists of a starting cone, a square and an end cone. A starts with a ball at the starting cone, B waits on the opposite side and C waits for the ball from B.

Execution
From a starting cone, A dribbles in a figure eight through the square and passes the ball to B. B takes the ball and dribbles back also in a figure eight and passes to C.

Coaching tip
This drill also includes the typical principles of large group training: two-footedness, frequent changes of direction, turning to the left and right, changing angles and high number of reps.

Variations
- To ensure that both feet are trained equally, the figure eight dribbling should also start from the left side.
- The turns can all be performed both to the right and to the left, thus changing the type and difficulty of the basic techniques at the cone.

Infinite Figure Eight Dribbling

Set-up
Course with three squares (or four or five, depending on the size of the group), each player has a ball.

Execution
The players dribble in one direction on the predetermined paths and then around the outside back to the starting point. If there are more than eight participants, the coach should increase the rows of the square to eliminate the waiting time at the starting cone.

Coaching tips
- It is important that the players know the running and dribbling paths so that they know what to do.
- The coach can easily keep an eye on the progress of the drill and easily correct the players.

Figure eight dribbling techniques
- kick with the inside/outside of the foot.
- 270 degree turn inwards/outwards.
- drag the ball back with the sole of the foot.
- drag back behind the standing leg.
- dummy step/step-over/scissors.

Variations
- start to the left.
- start to the right.

Figure Eight Dribbling with turning point

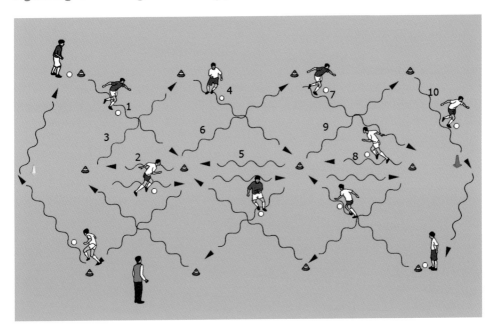

Set-up
Layout: 1-3-3-3-3-1, all players have a ball.

Execution
The players dribble in a figure eight through the first row of squares up to the last cone, then around the turning cone and back through the second row of squares.

Techniques in Figure Eight Dribbling
- kick with the inside/outside of the foot.
- 270 degree turn inwards/outwards.
- drag the ball back with the sole of the foot.
- drag back behind the standing leg.
- dummy step/step-over/scissors.

Coaching tip
The turning directions, changes of direction and techniques should be varied constantly.

Variations
- clockwise.
- counterclockwise.

3.5.2.7 Combinations

It's easy to combine large group training drills with infinite drills so that the angles vary within a drill and the players' orientation ability is challenged even more.

The following examples should encourage you to develop new drills. There are no limits to imagination. Changing and combining different drills ensures that boredom is never an issue and that the players always need to concentrate. The stimulus of new drills and the use of a variety of techniques support the learning process.

Combination 1: Comb and Zigzag

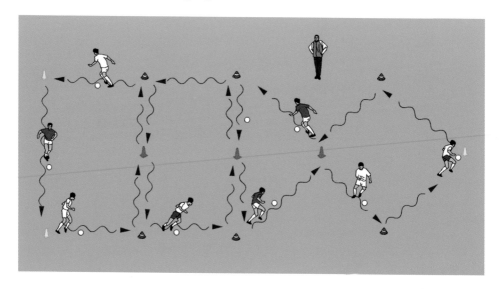

Set-up
Course combining the Comb and the Zigzag.

Execution
The illustration shows a combination of the Comb and the Zigzag. The players start with typical techniques as required by the Comb and change during the course of the drill to the Zigzag, where different techniques are required.

Variations
• clockwise.
• counterclockwise.

Combination 2: Zigzag and Comb

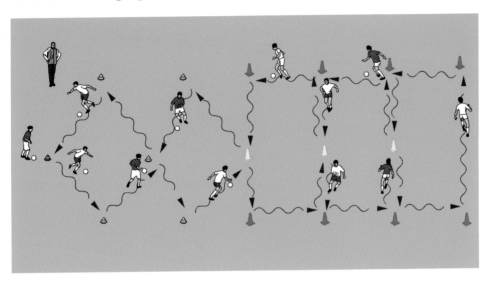

Set-up
Course combining the Zigzag and the Comb.

Execution
The illustration shows a combination of the Zigzag and the Comb. The players start with typical Zigzag techniques and change during the drill to the Comb, where different techniques are required.

Variations
- start to the right.
- start to the left.

Combination 3: Figure Eight Dribbling and Comb

Set-up
Course combining Figure Eight Dribbling and the Comb.

Execution
The illustration shows a combination of Figure Eight Dribbling and the Comb. The players start with typical techniques required for Figure Eight Dribbling and change during the drill to the Comb, where different techniques are solicited.

Variations
- start to the right.
- start to the left.

Zigzag with passing sequence

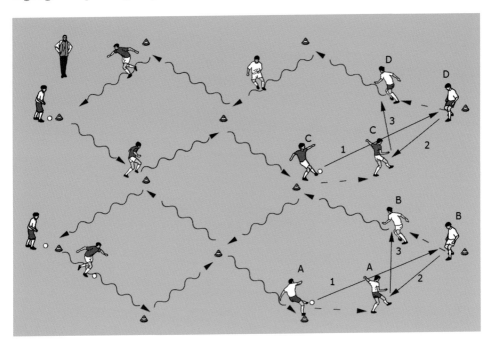

Set-up
Course with Quadruple Zigzag and follow-through action.

Execution
The players dribble through the Zigzag. A player waits without a ball at the last cone (5-10 yards away from the Zigzag). The dribbler performs a passing sequence with him, takes his place and waits for the next player.

Coaching tip
Infinite drills for large groups can also be combined with other additional drills. These follow-through actions can be included in large group training:

- passes.
- coordination drills.
- shots at the goal.

Zigzag with shots at the goal

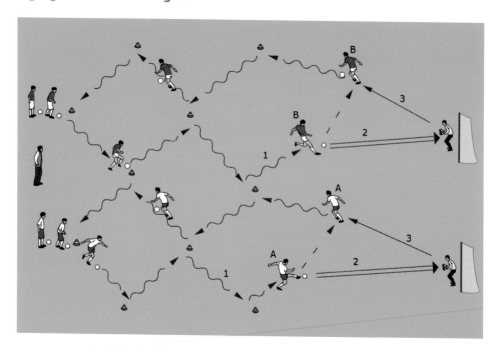

Set-up
Course with Quadruple Zigzag and shot at the goal.

Execution
The players dribble through the Zigzag. Behind the end cone (10-20 yards away from the Zigzag) are mini-goals or normal goals with goalkeeper. The dribbler shoots after the Zigzag to the goal, takes his ball and dribbles back to the start.

Coaching tips
- Drills involving shooting at the goal are always very motivating for children.
- Another additional task could involve the player outplaying an opponent before shooting at the goal. After shooting at the goal, the player dribbles back down the preset path and completes another task on the other side. It is important that the infinite drill is not too long, so that the players are not too tired when they come to shoot at the goal.
- The advantage of this drill is that no player waits to shoot at the goal, but repeats basic movements.

Comb with coordination drills

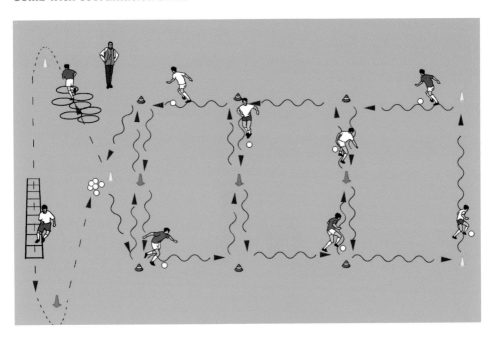

Set-up
Course with Comb (or other large group drill) followed by coordination course.

Execution
Follow the large group drill with a coordination training course with rods, tires, hurdles or coordination ladders. (see the DVD 'Coordination Training for Schools and Clubs'). The players leave their ball in the designated area, complete a coordination task and then return to dribbling training.

Coaching tips
• The coach should ensure that the training load is evenly spread throughout the coordination course and include sufficient rest periods.
• Functional gymnastics creates the necessary recovery breaks and prevents one-sided loading.

3.5.3   Opponent from Behind

An attacker waits for the ball from a teammate, stands with his back to the goal and is closely marked by an opponent. A very unpleasant situation! The player cannot see his opponent's reactions and feels very stressed. Beginners in particular get nervous, make mistakes and lose the ball.

The attacker has four ways of reacting to the ball passed to him.

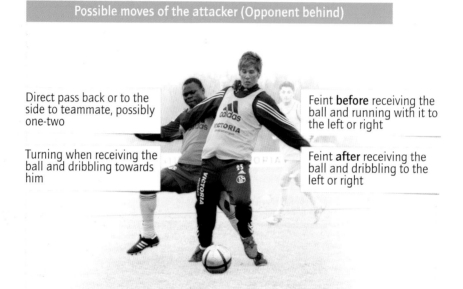

Possible moves of the attacker (Opponent behind)

Direct pass back or to the side to teammate, possibly one-two

Turning when receiving the ball and dribbling towards him

Feint **before** receiving the ball and running with it to the left or right

Feint **after** receiving the ball and dribbling to the left or right

Possible moves with the opponent behind

3.5.3.1   Possible Moves with the Opponent Behind

1. Direct pass back or to the side to teammate, possibly one-two
The attacker plays the ball directly back or to the side and shakes off the opponent (with the aid of a feint). This can also lead to a one-two. A covert pass is very effective as it makes it very difficult for the defender to take possession of the ball.

2. Turning when receiving the ball
The player sprints toward the ball, thus shaking off the opponent. As he receives the ball, he turns toward the opponent and then dribbles toward him. A feint before the sprint misleads the opponent, thus giving the attacker a slight time advantage.

3. Feint before directly picking up the ball

Feints (e.g., dummy step) are very effective and successful before picking up the passed ball. The opponent is wrong-footed; the attacker dribbles the ball in the opposite direction, while taking care not to lose possession of the ball. It is particularly dangerous when the ball is passed at a very sharp angle. The ball should be picked up covertly and close to the body, which allows the attacker to shield the ball to protect it in case a defender tackles.

Taking the ball and running with it directly with the outside of the foot

The player shields the approaching ball with his body and runs with it with the outside of his right foot on the move.

Taking the ball and running with it directly with the inside of the foot

4. Feint after receiving the ball

It can happen that an attacker has the ball at his feet and is attacked by an opponent behind him. He shields the ball with his body, uses a single or double feint and dribbles past the defender. The feint can be preceded by slowly guiding the ball to the side so that the opponent is enticed out of his stable position into a running movement and is even more surprised by the following sudden change of direction.

Step-over and receipt of the ball with the inside of the foot

3.5.3.2   Practice: Drills with the Opponent Behind

The following preliminary drills are a good way of preparing for game situations where the opponent comes from behind.

The players learn to control the ball even under pressure, to take their eyes off the ball and to perceive the opponent's reactions, even when the opponent is behind them.

a) Solo Drills

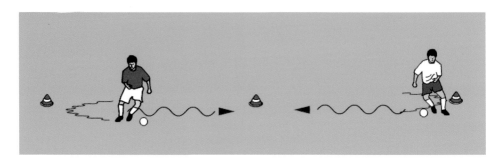

Set-up
In this solo drill, each player has two cones 3-4 yards apart and a ball.

Execution
The players dribble sideways between cones that are 3-5 yards apart. This drill automates the basic movements that are necessary to trick an opponent coming from behind.

Techniques
- Kicking with the inside/outside of the foot, then alternating the two.
- scissors/step-over/dummy step.
- drag the ball behind the standing leg.

Coaching tip
The players learn to move the ball confidently to the side, to shield it and to change direction.

b) Partner Drills

Set-up
In this partner drill, each player has two cones (3-4 yards apart) and a ball.

Execution
The players dribble in pairs between cones that are 3-4 yards apart. The partner's presence simulates the pressure that an attacker feels when an opponent is behind him/her.

Techniques
- kicking with the inside/outside of the foot, then alternating the two.
- scissors/step-over/dummy step.
- drag the ball behind the standing leg.

Coaching tips
- The opponent is passive at first, and just runs alongside the player, then puts gentle pressure on the player.
- This teaches the players to safely move the ball sideways and to shield it and to change direction.

c) Drills in groups of three

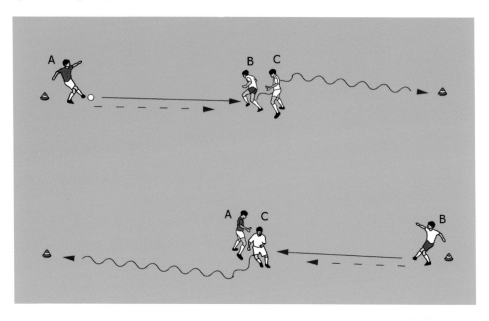

Set-up
Groups of three with two cones (9-13 yards apart), one ball per group of three.

Execution
A (passer) passes to B (attacker), B receives the ball, dummies C, dribbles around C and dribbles to the next cone. A sprints to C and becomes his opponent. Now B is the passer, C the dribbler and A the opponent. B passes to C, who receives the ball, dummies A and dribbles to the next cone. B sprints to A and becomes the defender. Now C is the passer, A the dribbler and B the opponent.

Coaching tips
- This is a very realistic drill to simulate game situations where the opponent comes from behind in groups of three.
- The advantage of this drill lies in the change of tasks for the players. Each completes successively the task of passer, dribbler and opponent.
- This drill is also suitable for practicing directly taking the ball and running with it.

Pass – Controlling and shielding the ball – Feints

d) Goal-scoring Drills

Once the players have mastered the basic drills, they should also use them in a drill with a follow-through action (shot at the goal or cross). This enables the players to understand the purpose of the basic drills and see them in the context of a match situation.

Pass, feint and shot at the goal

To start with, the opponent acts only as an orientation aid and partner who goes along with the feints. This enables the dribbler to gain self-assurance and become more and more confident in performing the feints he/she has learned. The better the attacker masters the techniques, the greater the resistance of the defender should be. Advanced players genuinely fight for the ball. In the **first stage**, the players first receive the ball before they trick the opponent and dribble past him. They should practice scissors, step-overs, dummy steps and dragging the ball behind the standing leg with freedom and creativity.

In the **second stage**, the dribbler also dribbles forward with the ball that is passed to him/her past the opponent toward the goal. Beforehand, he/she deceives the defender with a dummy step in the opposite direction. Beginners try out the direction first and the opponent (partner) reacts in the desired way. The role of the defender could also be taken by the coach. Advanced players should master both sides and be able to shake off/outplay the opponent who reacts as though in a real game.

Opponent behind with shot at the goal

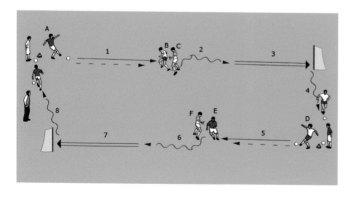

Set-up

Two mini goals, 10-12 players, infinite set-up: passing, dribbling, shot at the goal and back on the other side.

Execution

On two sides, one player passes to the center player, who is marked from behind by an opponent. After performing a feint and then dribbling for a short distance, the dribbler shoots at the mini goal and then goes to stand on the other side at the end of the row.

Variations

- stronger defense.
- two normal goals with goalkeeper.

3.5.4   Use in Game Situations

So that the players become not only drills world champions but also successful match dribblers, they should practice the acquired basic moves not only in closed drills such as the Zigzag or Figure Eight Dribble, but also apply them in game situations even in the very early stages. It will then be clear to the players right from the start why they should be able to master these basic techniques in their sleep. After an intensive drills phase, the coach always gives his players the opportunity to use the acquired techniques creatively.

Often a single feint is not enough to shake off an opponent, in which case the player performs a second feint and wins the tackle.

3.5.4.1   **Zidane Turn**

Opponent from the side
One player dribbles up to a marker, steps briefly on the ball and drags it back quickly in the opposite direction. This move is important for a winger who is starting to make a run up the wing and is under pressure from a defender. The attacker makes a lunging movement to a cross, stops it and drags the ball back. Then he passes to the side or plays a wide ball to the other wing or, after dribbling around the defender lying on the ground, takes a shot at the goal.

3.5.4.2   Use in Tackles

An opponent attacks from the side and would like to take the ball from the dribbler. The opponent tries to block the kick with another step towards the ball. The dribbler interrupts the kicking action and suddenly and unexpectedly drags the ball backwards. He/she takes advantage of the short time that the opponent needs to react to this change of direction and dribbles quickly in the new direction, thus gaining time and space to make a pass, take a shot at the goal or dribble unchallenged into the free space.

Variations
- opponent on the right.
- opponent on the left.

3.5.4.3   Game Situations on the Wing

Sprint down the wing, attacks by the opponent, interruption of movement + shot feint, pass to a midfielder.

3.5.4.4   Game Situation on the Halfway Line

Tackle on the halfway line, interrupt feint and break, pass to partner in the midfield, take the ball and run with it, breakaway over the halfway line.

3.5.5   Use in Small Competitions and Game Forms

The players should often be given the chance to use the acquired techniques in small games and matches. The creative use of difficult techniques in game situations with active opponents requires a large repertoire of different moves. The incorporation of simple basic moves into more complex drills is vital for creating the foundation for a learning process that enables the players to use them later in matches. The games 1v1, 2v2 or odd-sided matches (e.g. 2v3) force players to dribble with feints.

3.5.5.1 Shaking Off an Opponent with a Shot at the Goal

Set-up
Two turning cones and two target cones, two mini goals 10 yards apart (or two normal goals with goal keeper), players are organized in pairs with a ball.

Execution
A dribbler and a defender stand in the middle of two cones 4-6 yards apart. The dribbler tries to shake off the defender with a quick sequence of feints. If he succeeds, and reaches the outside cone on time, he shoots the ball at the mini goal. Then it is the next pair's turn.

Coaching tips
* A skilled attacker unbalances his opponent or misleads him into stepping to the side and uses this small time advantage.
* He now has a clear path to shoot at the goal.
* He must shield the ball all the time, because if the defender kicks the ball away, they swap roles.

3.5.5.2   1v1 Playing Down the Line

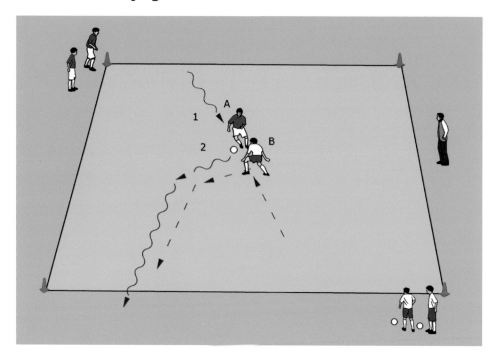

Set-up
Rectangle 6 x 8 yards, four cones, 1v1.

Execution
In a rectangle measuring 6 x 8 yards, two players play 1v1. The goal is the whole line between the two cones on the opposite side. A goal is valid if the attacker dribbles the ball over the line. The defender then receives the ball and becomes the attacker. The game should not last too long (max. 1 minute) so that the players do not get too tired. A change of competition and recovery exercises (such as juggling) allow the players to recover.

3.5.5.3   2v2 Playing Down the Line

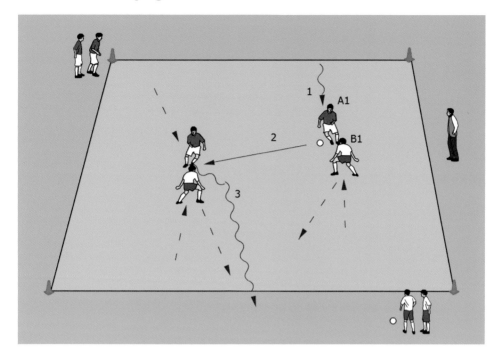

Set-up
Playing area: rectangle 8-12 yards, 2v2 over target lines, four cones, a ball and two marking vests for every four players.

Execution
The game is played 2v2 over 2 lines. There are more variations than for the 1v1, for both players in a team can both dribble and pass to a partner. There are many tackle situations in which the attacker can try out the acquired feints and their dribbling skills.

Other game formations
* 1v2
* 2v3
* 3v3
* 3v4

3.5.5.4   1v1 to Four Small Goals

Set-up
Rectangle 12 x 6 yards with two small goals on each long side.

Execution
The game is played 1v1. Each team consists of two players, of which one is always resting. A substitution is possible at any time, but no later than 45 seconds after the start. The players try, by skillful dribbling and a variety of feints, to set up a fast break to one of the two goals. A goal is only valid if the player dribbles the ball with the feet over the goal line. Playing time: 2-3 minutes.

Coaching tips
* When organizing a tournament, add active recovery breaks between substitutions because this competition is very tiring.
* The size of the playing field and the goals depends on the age and ability of the players.

3.5.5.4   4v4 in Doubled Penalty Area

Set-up
Game 4v4 with two goals and goalkeeper in doubled penalty area.

Execution
Free game with two goals and goalkeeper. In a narrow space, the players have ample opportunity to put their acquired feints into practice in order to arrive at a shooting position. This game features a combination of quick passing and tackling.

Variation
Goals that follow successful dribbling are worth double, which encourages risk-taking and a willingness to seek out tackles.

4 PASSING

Perfect ball control also means being able to finish off an action precisely. The pass is the most frequent soccer action and the basic element for every team game, as it creates the connection between the players on a team. Other types of follow-through action are the shot at the goal and the cross.

4.1 Basic Theory

Ball control and passing have a lot in common, which is why many ball control drills are also suitable for passing training.

Players should be able to play a variety of passes:
* with the inside and outside of the foot, the full instep or the inside instep, the head and the heel.
* diagonally, at a steep angle, across or backwards.
* with or without bending the ball.
* straight to the foot or into free space at the correct pace.
* as a one-two or pass via a third person.
* as a high ball over an opponent or through a gap between two or more players.

Lob over the opponent's feet

Game-specific and two-footed training

The pace of modern soccer often leaves the player no time to bring the ball under control and change to his/her preferred kicking leg. Players who can pass with the right and left feet speed up the game and have more chances to shoot at the goal. The passing always has a tactical context, which is why the drills should be combined with other emphases (running into a free space, triangle formation, making use of 2v1 situations, changing position, etc).

Coaching points for passing training

- Orient passing accuracy and sharpness to the game situation.
- Low passes are faster and easier to control than high ones.
- The timing of the pass is crucial.
- Include a dummy run before trapping the ball in order to confuse the opponent.
- Pass to the foot furthest away from the opponent.
- Depth is more important than width.
- Good verbal and non-verbal communication between players (eye contact between pass giver and pass receiver).

Correction tips

- Kick the center of the ball for a low pass and the bottom of the ball for a lob.

- Pass with momentum instead of with force.

- The pass with the inside of the foot is the safest and most accurate, but also the easiest to read. The pass with the outside of the foot is more discreet and requires almost no preparation, but is technically more difficult due to the significantly smaller hitting surface of the ball.

Targeted long ball

4.2   Drills for Beginners

4.2.1   Partner Drill 1 (with Ball)

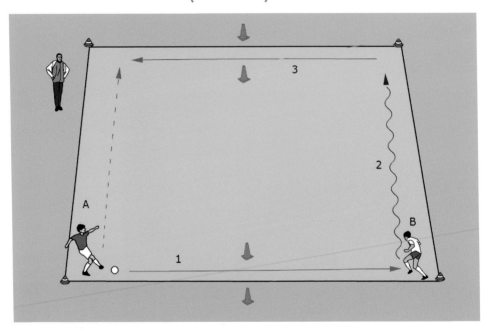

Set-up
A square with sides 5-8 yards in length, one cone goal on two parallel sides (cones 1-2 yards apart), one ball per pair.

Execution
A passes through the goal to B, who takes the ball directly to the side and dribbles to the other side, where B passes through the other goal back to A.

Variations
• Turn to both left and right
• Pass with both left and right feet
• Vary the gaps between the cones

Observation points
• Well-timed and accurate passes.
• control the ball and run with it in a counterclockwise direction with the inside of the left foot/outside of the right foot.
• Flowing rhythm of ball control from dribble to pass.
• Increase the pace of the pass sequences and flowing execution of the drill.

4.2.2   Partner Drill 2 (with Two Balls)

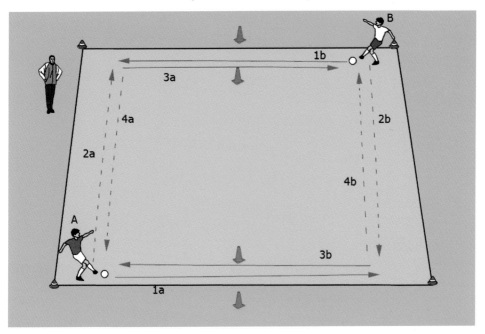

Set-up
A square with sides 5-8 yards in length, one cone goal on two parallel sides (cones 1-2 yards apart), two balls per pair.

Execution
A plays a well-timed pass through the goal to B's side and at the same time, B passes through the other goal to A. Both sprint to the ball and control it before passing it back again.

Variations
- Turn to both left and right.
- Pass with both left and right feet.
- Vary the gaps between the cones.
- Play direct passes.

Observation points
- Well-timed and accurate passes.
- Increase the pace of the pass sequences and flowing execution of the drill with good coordination between the partners.

4.2.3   Infinite Passing in a Square (Groups of Five)

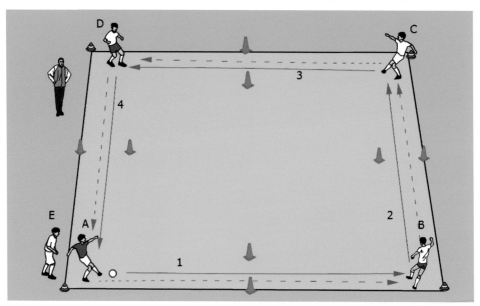

Set-up
A square with sides of 6-10 yards in length, with one cone goal on each side (gap of 1-2 yards between the cones), one ball per group of five.

Execution
A makes a well-timed pass through the goal to B, who passes the ball with two touches to C. C passes through the next goal to D, who passes with two touches to E. Each player runs after their ball and then waits at the next cone.

Variations
• Turn clockwise/counterclockwise.
• Pass with both left and right feet.
• Vary the gaps between the cones.
• Play direct passes.
• Getting into position to receive the pass.
• Play with two balls at the same time at the diagonal starting points (higher repetition rate and quicker orientation).

Observation points
• Well-timed and accurate passes.
• Increase the pace of the passing sequences and flowing execution of the drill.

4.2.4   Passing in a Triangle

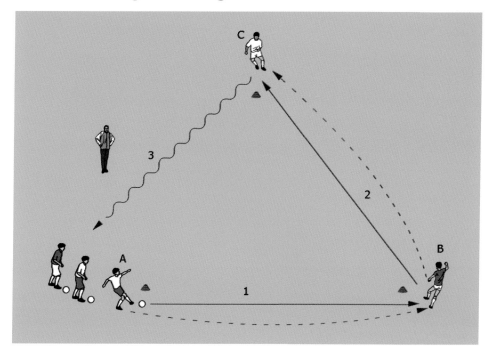

Set-up
One player (without a ball) stands at each cone of the triangle. 3-5 players wait at the starting cone with a ball.

Execution
A passes to B, who controls the ball and passes to C (two touches). C controls the ball and dribbles quickly back to the starting position. Each player runs after their ball and stands at the next cone.

Variations
- Direct pass from position B.
- Start in both directions.
- Include dummy runs.
- Vary the gaps between the cones.

Observation points
- Well-timed and accurate passes.
- Increase the pace of the passing sequences and flowing execution of the drill.

4.2.5   Passing into Player's Path

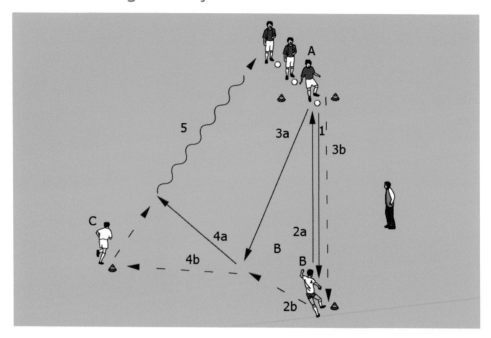

Set-up
Two players stand without a ball at the first two cones of a triangle (side lengths: 6-10 yards). 3-5 players with a ball stand at the third cone.

Execution
A passes to B, who passes directly back and makes him/herself available to receive a lateral pass. A passes into the path of B and takes over his/her position. B passes into the path of C and runs to the vacated cone. C controls the ball and dribbles to the end of the group. The next player passes to A, etc.

Variations
• Start the drill in both directions.
• Include dummy runs.
• Vary the gaps between the cones.

Observation points
• Well-timed and accurate passing.
• Bring the ball safely under control before starting to dribble without changing rhythm.
• Increase the pace of the passing sequences and flowing execution of the drill.

4.3   Drills for Advanced Players

4.3.1   Give and Go in a Triangle

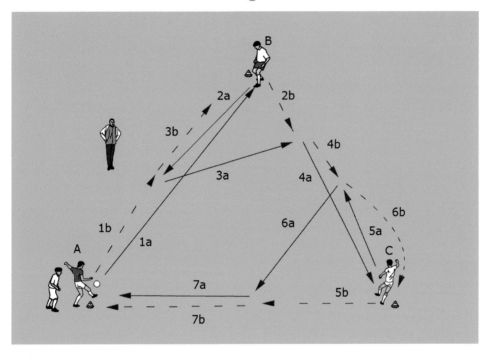

Set-up
A player without a ball stands at each of the first two cones of a triangle (side length 6-10 yards). Two players with one ball stand at the third cone.

Execution
A passes to B and then plays a give and go with B, B passes the ball directly to C and then plays a give and go with C. The players run after their ball to the next cone.

Coaching tips
- In this drill, the passing sequence goes: **forward – backward – into the player's path.**
- It involves varying between sharply played pressure passes, sensitively played balls and well-timed balls into the path of a player.
- This drill should also be performed in a counterclockwise direction.

4.3.2   Direct Passing in a Diamond – Basic Drill

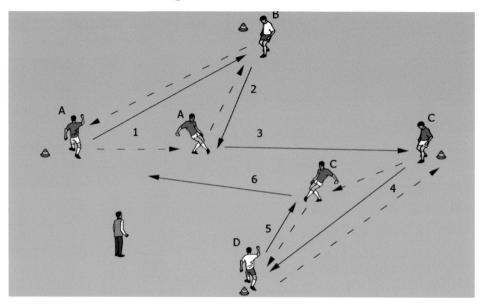

Set-up
A diamond marked out with four cones, one ball per group of four.

Execution
A passes to B and sprints to the center of the diamond, B passes into the path of A, who passes directly to C. A and B swap places. C passes directly (or after quickly controlling the ball) to D and sprints to the center of the diamond, D passes into the path of C, who passes directly to B. C and D swap places.

Coaching tips
* Passers and give and go players continually swap places.
* Aim for correct running and passing paths, passing sharpness and accuracy (accuracy takes precedence over sharpness).
* The passer should pass to the outside of the give and go player's foot (imaginary opponent behind).
* If the ball hasn't been passed accurately, it is better to control it first and then play on (allow several touches if necessary).
* The players must not lose concentration and must communicate well with each other.

Variations
* Pass to the right side.
* Introduce dummy runs.
* The give and go players break free towards the player who receives the ball.
* The passers kick from the ankle with the outside of the foot.

4.3.3   Direct Passing in a Diamond (Variation 1)

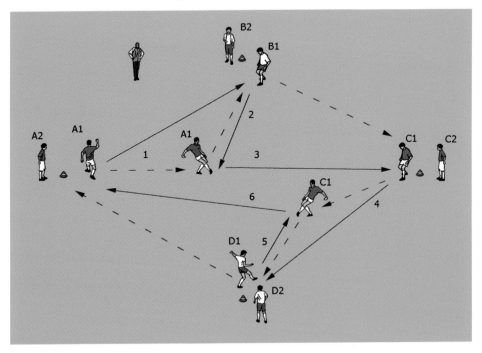

Set-up
A diamond marked out with four cones, one ball per group of eight.

Execution
A passes to B and sprints to the center of the diamond, B passes into the path of A and runs to position C, A passes directly to C and takes B's place, C passes directly to D and sprints to the center of the diamond, D passes into C's path and runs to position A, C passes direct to A2 and takes D's place.

Variation
Pass to the right side.

Coaching tip
The path of the give and go player is different to that in the basic form: the give and go player does not change places with the passer but sprints towards the next passer.

4.3.4 Direct Pass in a Diamond – One-Two

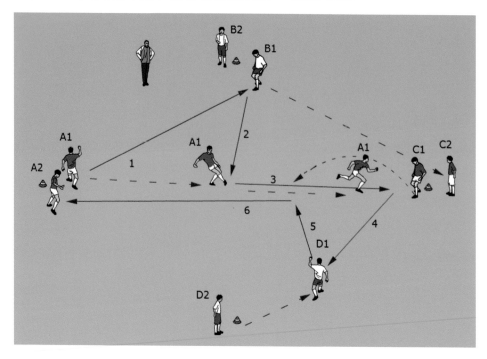

Set-up
A diamond marked out with four cones, one ball per group of eight.

Execution
A1 passes to B1 and sprints to the center of the diamond, B1 passes into the path of A1 and runs to position C, A1 passes direct to C1 and sprints towards them, C1 plays a one-two pass with D1, runs around A1 who is sprinting towards them, D1 passes into the path of C1 and runs to position A, C1 passes direct to A2 and sprints as an opponent to A2.

Variations
* Pass to the right side.
* Instead of the one-two, the passer only pretends to perform a one-two and dribbles past the attacker.

Coaching tips
* The passer only plays a direct pass if the attacking player has sprinted near enough. Otherwise he plays a one-two only after quickly controlling the ball.
* Include dummy runs.

4.3.5   Zigzag Passing Game

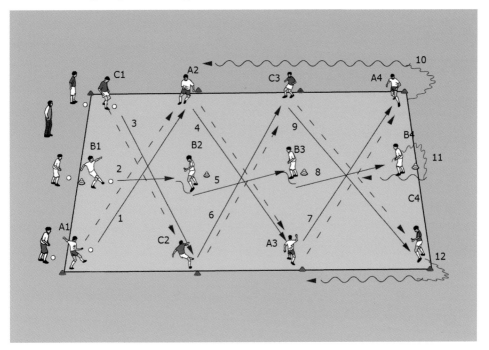

Set-up
Red and blue cones in a zigzag format 8-12 yards apart on the outside and yellow cones in the center, players stand at the start with the ball and a player without a ball stands at each of the other cones.

Execution
The players in group A pass their ball diagonally to the next player (A2, A3, A4) after quickly controlling it. The passer runs after his/her ball and takes over the position of the pass-receiver. The players in group C do exactly the same thing, but with a time-delay and crosswise. The first center player (B1) play a steep diagonal pass to B2, who controls the ball and after a quick turn (opponent behind situation) passes to the next player. The last player dribbles through the center to the starting cone.

Coaching tips
* The number of ball touches and the distance between the cones depend on the ability of the players and the training emphasis.
* Depending on the situation in the playing field, the passing should be quick and accurate.
* Accuracy takes precedence over pace.

Variations
- The groups swap over systematically (A becomes B, B becomes C and C becomes A).
- Opponents wait behind the pass-receivers (opponents then become the next pass receivers).
- Include dummy runs.

Training emphases
- The training of perception and the ability to read the game.
- Communication between passer and pass-receiver.
- Open body position of the pass-receiver.

Three stages to the target drill

As this drill represents a great challenge for the players' orientation ability, it is advisable to build up gradually to the target drill.

Stage 1: Dribbling for orientation

The players dribble to get their bearings, first from their starting cone to the prearranged cone, then back to the start and then they move on to the next color.

Stage 2: Passing with ball control

The number of touches of the ball depends on the situations in the center (3, 2 or direct) – but the important thing is to pass as soon as possible.

Stage 3: Passing as soon as possible

Pass as soon as possible (situation-dependent, if a player is in the way, the ball must briefly be controlled, then quickly passed on).

4.4 Drills

4.4.1 Odd-sided Passing

4.4.1.1 3v1 Basic Drill

Set-up
Square 6 x 6 yards (size dependant on ability), three players outside and one player in the center.

Execution
Three outside players pass the ball to each other freely around the square, the inside player tries to touch the ball, then the outside player who loses the ball goes into the center.

Variations
• free passing.
• two touches.
• direct passing.

Coaching tips
• Correct running into a free space, always creating two passing points.
• Skilled defending by the defenders, forcing passing errors.

4.4.1.2   3v1 Field Change 1 (3+1 v 1)

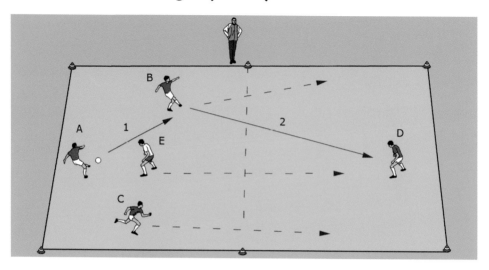

Set-up
Two rectangles 4 x 6 yards, 3v1 in the left rectangle, one player can be passed to in the second rectangle.

Execution
The players play 3v1 in the left rectangle. In the other outside rectangle, there is an additional player in the team. After a successful pass to the outside player, two outside players and the inside player move up to play 3v1. If the inside player touches the ball, the player who has made the mistake must go into the center.

Variations
- Two touches.
- Direct passing.

Coaching tips
- The free player should wait for the ball as far back as possible to allow the opponent very little chance of winning the ball and to give the teammates time to get into position.
- Training goals are: shifting the game and moving up, triangle formation and passing deep.
- Skillful defensive play by the defenders, forcing passing errors.

4.4.1.3   4v2 Basic Drill

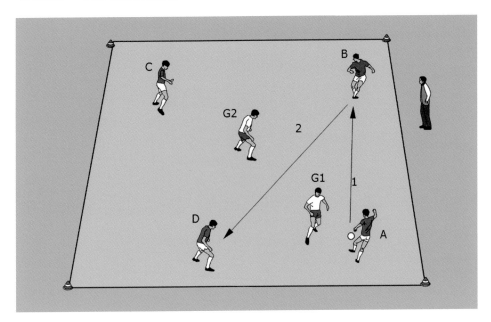

Set-up
Square 10 x 10 yards, four players on the outside and 2 players in the center.

Execution
The four outside players pass the ball freely to each other around the square while the two inside players try to touch the ball. The outside player who makes a mistake then goes into the center. The player who stays longest in the center goes to the outside.

Variations
- Free passing.
- Two touches of the ball.
- Direct passes.
- Defenders must tackle hard to get the ball.
- Defenders must pass the ball to each other once.

Coaching tips
- Running correctly into a free space.
- Spotting and making good use of gaps.
- Accurate passing.
- Skillful play by the defenders and provoking passing mistakes.

4.4.1.4   4v2 Game Shift 1 (4v2 + 2)

Set-up
Two squares 10 x 10 yards, 4v2 in the left square, two players can be passed to in the second square.

Execution
The players play 4v2 in the left square. In the other outside square there are two other players. After a successful pass to one player in the other square, two outside players and the two inside players move up to play 4v2. If an inside player touches the ball, the player who has made the mistake must go into the center. The player who is in the center the longest goes to the outside.

Variations
*   Two touches of the ball.
*   Direct passes.

Coaching tips
*   Running correctly into free spaces.
*   Spotting and making the most of gaps.
*   Accurate passing.
*   Game shifting and moving up.
*   Triangle formation and playing long balls.
*   Skillful play by the defenders and the forcing of passing errors.

4.4.1.5   4v2 Game Shift 2 (4v2 +1 +1)

Set-up
Three squares 10 x 10 yards, 4v2 in the middle square, one player waiting to receive passes in each outside square.

Execution
4 players play against 2 in the middle square. One player stands in each of the two outside squares as far as possible from the middle square. After a successful pass to the outside player, three outside players and both center players move up to form a new 4v2 game. Whoever makes a mistake goes into the middle. If a middle player touches the ball, the player who has made the mistake must go into the center. The player who is in the middle the longest goes to the outside.

Variations
• Two touches of the ball.
• Direct passes.

Coaching tips
• Running correctly into free spaces.
• Spotting and making the most of gaps.
• Accurate passing.
• Game shifting and moving up.
• Triangle formation and playing long balls.
• Skillful play by the defenders and the forcing of passing errors.

4.4.1.6   6v4 in the Outside Square

Set-up
Team A has 6 players around the outside of a 15 x 15 yard square (size depends on the age and ability of the players); team B has 4 players inside the square.

Execution
Team A gets one point for every pass through the square to another outside player. Team B tries to stop this by skillful space play to gain possession of the ball. After a predetermined time, four of the outside players swap places with the inside players.

Variation
• Competition around the center circle.

Coaching tips
• Quick spotting of gaps and targeted sharp passing to center players.
• Choose the size of the square to allow for an equal balance between the outside players making successful passing and the inside players winning the ball.

4.4.1.7   6v4 in a Rectangle

Set-up
Rectangle 20 x 15 yards, team A has six players and team B has four players.

Execution
Team A gets one point for a certain number of passes (e.g. 10). B tries to stop them by skillful defending. If the smaller team wins the ball, they retain possession as long as possible to play for time.

Variations
- Players in the larger team are allowed to touch the ball twice.
- Direct passing by the smaller team.

Coaching tips
- Quick and accurate passing taking as few risks as possible.
- Creating many passing opportunities by good player distribution and intelligent running into free spaces.
- Spotting and making good use of gaps.
- The larger team should also occupy the center.

4.4.2   Odd-sided Games with Neutral Players

4.4.2.1   1v1 + 2 with Two Neutral Players

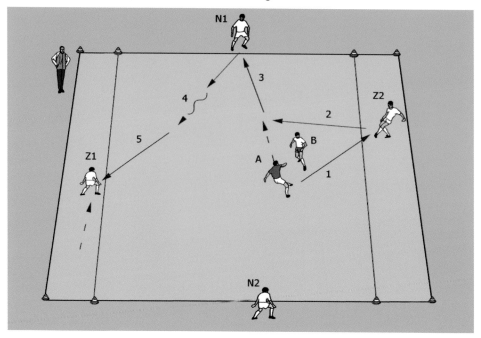

Set-up
Square 10 x 10 yards (or rectangle 8 x 16 yards); 1v1 plus two neutral players and two target players.

Execution
Players play 1 against 1 in a square, with two additional neutral players who make themselves available for passes on both sidelines. Two target players stand at each side of the top of the rectangle. Each pass to a target player is worth one point. A pass to the same target player is only valid if the ball was previously passed either to the neutral players or across the center of the playing area.

Variations
• Neutral players pass directly.
• 2v2 (field: 15 x 15 yards).
• 3v3 (field: 20 x 20 yards).
• 4:4 (field: 25 x 25 yards).

Coaching tips
• Include sufficient active recovery phases.
• The players swap roles regularly.
• After passing to the neutral players, immediately leave the marking shadow.
• Start into free space.

4.4.2.2   2v2 + 4 Neutral Players in the Corners

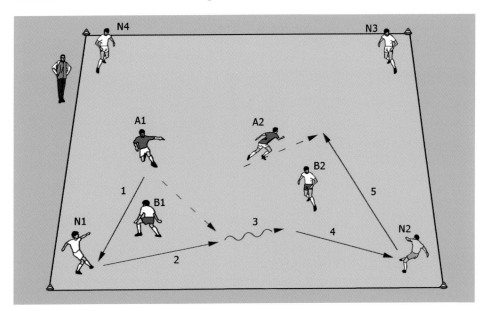

Set-up
Square 16 x 16 yards (rectangle 11 x 22 yards); 2v2 + 4 neutral players in the corners of the square.

Execution
The game is played 2v2 + 4 neutral players in the corners. The aim is to retain possession of the ball for as long as possible. Measure how long it takes the defenders to gain possession of the ball. If someone makes a mistake (touching the ball, or the ball going out), possession of the ball is awarded to the other team.

Playing time: one minute, then the two neutral players move to the inside and the inside players move outside.

Variations
• Passes with the four neutral players are counted.
• 3v3.
• 4v4.

Coaching tips
• This game is very tiring, so the players' roles should constantly be changed.
• Rests should be active (juggling, exercises).
• After passing to the neutral player, immediately leave the marking shadow.
• Start into free space.

4.5   Small Competitions

4.5.1   Dribblers against Passers

Set-up
One team (passers) has a ball and the players spread out evenly along the short sides of a 6 x 2 yard rectangle (size depends on the training focus and the players' ability), while the players of the other team (dribblers) each have a ball and stand at the start of a 6 x 10 yard rectangle.

Execution
After the starting signal, the players of the first team pass the ball as quickly as possible back and forth between the goals and sprint to the other side. Each touch of the ball is worth one point. The players of the second team all dribble at the same time around the rectangle. When the last player has reached the end, the coach stops counting the passes. Passing the ball inside the rectangle is not allowed.

Variations
- Vary the gaps between the goal cones and the distances.
- Vary the dribbling tasks (slalom, dribbling techniques).

Coaching tips

- This game puts the player under time pressure when passing.
- It can be varied in many different ways and always combines a technical task with a conditioning task.
- The checking of the exact execution of the loading task should be very simple so that the coach can concentrate on counting the points for the technical task.

4.5.2   Passing around a Square

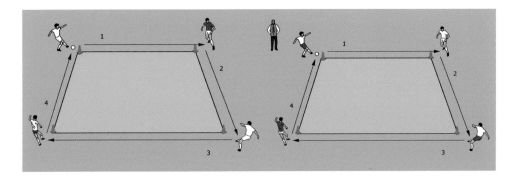

Set-up
Each team of four has one ball and a square with 4-7 yard long sides..

Execution
On a signal from the coach, the teams pass as quickly as possible around their square.
Which team makes the most passes or circuits during the given time (1-2 minutes)?
Which team is the first to complete a given number of circuits (2-5)?

Variations

- Passing clockwise/counterclockwise.
- Two touches of the ball are permitted.
- Professional version: only direct passes allowed (whoever does not pass the ball directly loses immediately).

Coaching tip
If the number of players is not divisible by four, the coach forms a triangle or a pentagon that has the same length sides as the square and can be completed in the same time.

4.5.3   Goal-pass Competition

Set-up
Every pair of players has a ball and a playing area with four cones situated 1-1.5 feet apart.

Execution
The game starts with a pass through the goal in the center. Each player can touch the ball twice. With the first touch, the pass receiver takes the ball to the side and with the second he passes the ball back to the other side. The players may not pass the ball back through the same goal. The first to reach 10 points wins the game.

A player is awarded one point if:
• The opponent touches the ball more than twice.

• The ball touches a cone.

• The opponent passes the ball back through the same goal.

Coaching tips
• Perception and being in the right place at the right time.

• Flowing, two-footed ball control and passing.
• React ability and anticipation.

Variations
• Vary the passing techniques.

• Tournament set-up: Champions League with promotion and demotion.

• Increase the number of goals (five cones – four goals).

4.5.4 Ball Driving

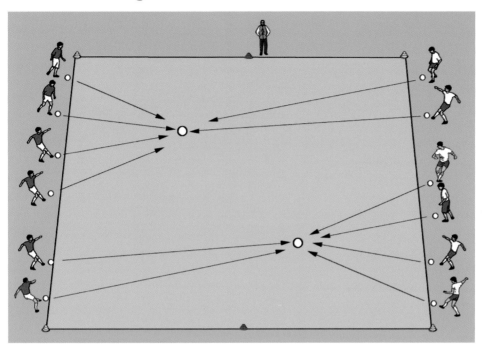

Set-up
In a limited space, two teams with balls stand opposite each other. In the center of the field lies, e.g., a light medicine ball.

Execution
Both teams try to kick the medicine ball over the opposite line with their balls. They may only stand outside the field. If a soccer ball lies within reach inside the field, they may quickly bring it outside. If a player stops the medicine ball with his foot, the opponent gets a point. The first to get three points wins the game.

Variation
The players throw with Swiss balls (volleyballs) and drive the medicine ball to the other side.

5 CROSSING

5.1 Basic Theory

Good crossing is trainable, but intensive practice and constant repetition are required to be able to play high quality crosses.

Crossing technique tips

- Attackers need to receive accurate, low crosses. The longer and higher a ball is passed, the more time defenders have to move in on the ball and the awaiting attacker.

- Crosses should be played on the run, not from a standing position.

- With the last touch before the cross, bring the ball towards you and turn the body inwards when planting the standing leg; the toes of the standing leg should also point inward.

Tips for making the most of crosses

- There must always be a player at the near and far posts!
- Strikers' timing: the strikers run across so that they can reach the ball about 5-10 yards before the goal running flat out and can kick the ball hard enough.
- The attackers should create options for the crosser in front of the goal by means of dummy runs and cross runs.
- Crosses should be made confidently and decisively.
- Be brave and fearless in heading duels (don't shut your eyes when heading the ball).
- Train to pass with both feet and from both sides.

5.2   Practice: Giving and Exploiting Crosses

5.2.1   Crossing Circuit

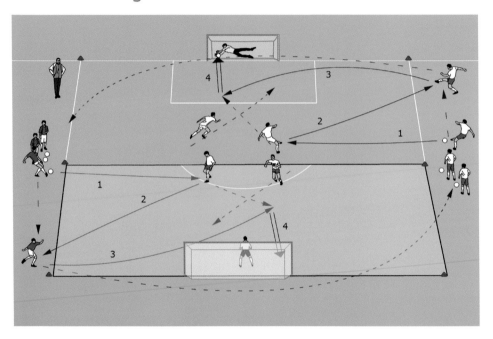

Set-up
Half a pitch, two goals with goalkeepers, two attackers in front of each goal, the other players spread out on both sides spread outside the pitch.

Execution
Both the first players in each group play a give and go with the attacker (1, 2) and cross from the goal line to the attackers (3) who cross over each other to get into a free space to receive the pass. The attacker converts the crosses as directly as possible (4). Then the cross players retrieve the ball and stand on the other side.

5.2.2   Crossing after Team Play with Partner

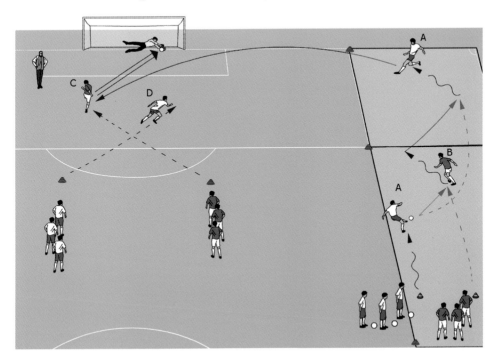

Set-up
Half a pitch, a goal with goalkeeper, two wingers for each run-through and two attackers in front of the goal with goalkeeper.

Execution
Wingers A and B pass to each other up to the goal line. Then one of the two wingers plays a cross to the two attackers C and D, who exploit the cross as well as possible. The next pair starts with two other forwards, and so on.

5.2.3 Crossing under Time Pressure

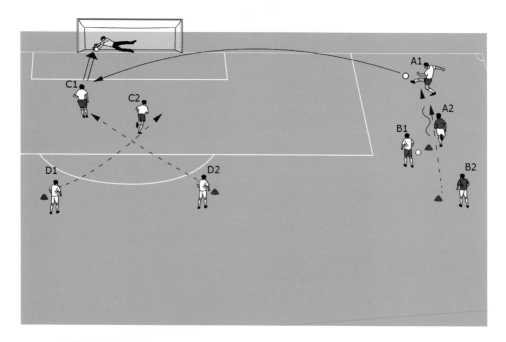

Set-up
The players pair up. The strikers stand in front of the penalty box and try to convert crosses into a goal with a goalkeeper. The pair of players stands one behind the other on the wing 2-5 yards apart (depending on their ability). The player in front has a ball.

Execution
The first pair of strikers (C1 and C2) awaits a cross from the winger A1, who dribbles up to the goal line, thus putting defender A2 under pressure. Then B1 crosses to D1 and D2, coming under pressure from B2 in the process. After five crosses, the players swap roles.

Variations
- Crossing from the left.
- Sharper, lower back pass from the goal line to the first post.

5.2.4 Crossing under Pressure from the Opponent

5.2.4.1 1v1 on the Wing with Cross

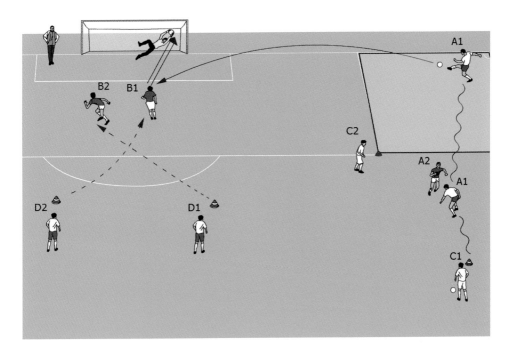

Set-up
Half a pitch, one goal with goalkeeper, mark a line level with the penalty area, outside the penalty area, the players are divided into two groups, two attackers wait to exploit the crosses in the penalty area.

Execution
A1 tries to deceive A2 with a feint, and to dribble past him down the wing. A2 can only follow him up to the continuation of the penalty area line. In front of the penalty area, attackers B1 and B2 await a cross from A1, who exploit it as directly as possible. The same sequence follows via C1 and C2 to D1 and D2.

Coaching tips
- The defenders are initially only partially active, thus giving the wingers a chance to cross.
- Wingers use different feints on the wing.

5.2.4.2 2v1 after Pass by Defender

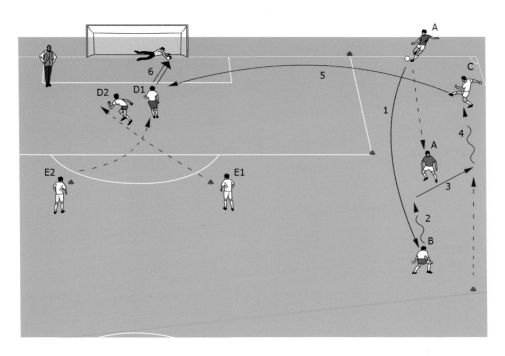

Set-up

Half-pitch, a goal with goalkeeper, two wingers, two forwards in front of the goal, one defender in the wing area on the goal line.

Execution

Defender A plays a high ball to wingers B and C and attacks them. B and C outplay A with a one-two and cross to forwards D1 and D2, who make the best possible use of the cross.

Coaching tip
*   Take advantage of the 2v1 situation on the wing.

5.2.4.3 5v5 Cross under Pressure from Opponent

Set-up
Half a pitch, a goal with goalkeeper and two counter-lines 44 yards in front of the goal, two passers with balls at the half-way line, three attackers and three defenders at the penalty area line and a defender outside in front of the counter-goal.

Execution
Passer A passes to winger B, who has a head start over defender C. Winger B brings the ball under control as fast as possible and crosses to the attacker in the middle. Passer A joins in the attacking play as an additional attacker alongside D, E and F. If the defending team succeeds in winning the ball, the defenders dribble across the counter-line.

5.2.5   Complex Crossing Drills

5.2.5.1   **Complex Wing Play Training**

Once wingers have mastered the technical and conditioning prerequisites, the next step is to coordinate the interaction between wingers. Game-specific passing sequences and attacking patterns on the wing are first practiced and automated without pressure from opponents. With increasing precision, opponents are included in the drills, as this kind of realistic, game-specific playing situation with time and opponent pressure is vital for developing tactical ability. In complex training drills, the players not only learn and automate the necessary techniques, but also important tactical solutions.

5.2.5.2   **Combination Play on the Wing**

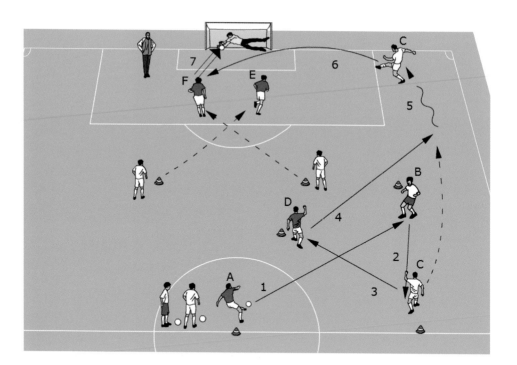

Set-up
Half a pitch, a goal with goalkeeper. Six players plus goalkeeper take part in an activity. Center midfielder A, right midfielder B, right full back C, center attacking midfielder D, two center forwards E and F.

Execution
A passes diagonally to B (1), who 'drips' the ball to C (2). C passes to D (3). D passes back to C (4), who runs behind B and makes himself available on the goal line. C crosses to the two center forwards E and F (6), who have just crossed over and go on to convert the direct cross (7).

5.2.6   Crossing in Game Forms

5.2.6.1   4v2 with Alternating Cross Players

Set-up
Playing field: about 44 yards x width of the soccer field, two teams with four players each, two cross-players on the wings.

Execution
This game form starts with a pass to the wing and a cross played into the box to the four players of the attacking team (blue). In front of every goal stand two defenders from the other team (red). If a goal is scored, the blue team retains possession of the ball and starts an attack to the other side against the two other red players who are waiting there. If the defenders gain possession of the ball or the goalkeeper catches the crossed ball, the red team passes to a cross-player and the red team starts an attack on the other goal.

Variation
The teams play 4v3, in which case only one player waits in the opponents' half of the field.

5.2.6.2 Game with Wing Zones

Set-up
Half a pitch, two goals with goalkeeper, two teams (7v7 or 8v8), two wing zones outside the penalty areas as extensions of the penalty box lines.

Execution
The game is played 7v7 with two or three touches of the ball in the center of the playing field and free play in the outfield. The outer areas are restricted to a maximum of two attackers and two defenders. Goals that are scored through the center are worth one point, while goals that are scored via a wing zone are worth three points.

Variation
The team in possession of the ball in the wing zone has more players than the other (2v1).

5.2.6.3   7v7 with Taboo Zone

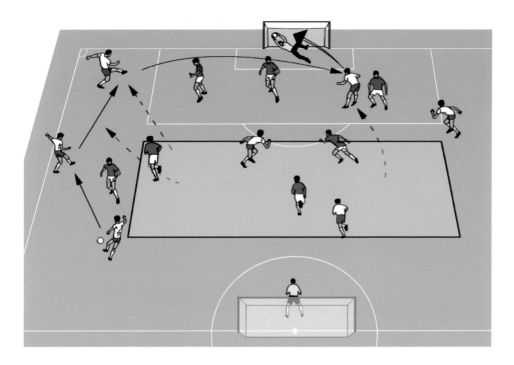

Set-up
Half a pitch with a taboo zone in the center, 7v7, each team has a goalkeeper.

Execution
Two teams play in one half of the pitch 7v7 with two goalkeepers in the large goal. There is a taboo zone in the center of the playing field. The ball must not be passed into or through the taboo zone, although players can run through it.

Any infraction of this rule means that the other team is given possession of the ball.

Coaching tips
• The taboo zone makes it more difficult to pass down the middle and encourages passing down the wing.
• The coach can change the way the team plays by varying the size and location of the taboo zone.

6 SHOOTING AT THE GOAL

6.1 Basic Theory

There are two types of training for shooting at the goal:
- goal shooting technique training
- game-specific goal-shooting training

Goal-shooting technique training is an important part of training for beginners, but top players should also regularly repeat basic goal shooting techniques under difficult conditions in order to be prepared for the stress of the match. The better the player, the more important it is to practice shooting at the goal under match conditions.

6.1.1 Goal shooting technique training

Goal shooting technique training entails laying the foundations for successful shooting at the goal by means of simple, age-appropriate drills. Frequent repetition allows the players to learn and improve all-important goal shooting techniques from different distances after dribbling, after trapping the ball and directly. They learn to judge ball movements correctly and how to bring their bodies into the correct position for receiving the ball.

The coach uses drills that enable him teach important shooting techniques as effectively as possible. The structure of the drills must allow players the necessary amount of repetition.

In goal shooting technique training, the coach should make sure that long waiting queues are avoided and use simple exercises. A complicated exercise only distracts the players' attention from the actual learning goal.

Effective goal shooting technique meets the following criteria:
- A high number of reps and high exercise intensity allows the players to learn and improve their goal shooting techniques. This can be done with small group activities and as much shooting at the goal as possible.
- The coach corrects and helps to remedy postural errors (upper body, foot position, recovery movement) and tactical errors (incorrect position on the ball, non-optimal running path, incorrect change of pace).
- The players practice shooting directly at the goal near to the goal and shots with a second touch from different positions.
- Players should also practice the exploitation of rebounds.

6.1.2 Game-specific Goal Shooting Training

- Drills in and around the penalty box are ideally suited to the practice and game-specific application of all important technical and tactical aspects of shooting at the goal
- The pressure of space, opponent, time and accuracy must be gradually increased in a way that is age and ability-appropriate.
- Small goal shooting competitions increase motivation and are both important and effective. Group pressure adds to the competitive atmosphere and fun factor.

Distance and size of the playing area
The distance to goal and the size of the playing field are important in all learning stages. The coach chooses these according to the age and ability of his players and to the objectives of the goal shooting training:

- Shooting from close range (area between the goal area and the 12 yard box).
- Shooting from mid-range (area from the 12 yard box to the edge of the penalty area).
- Shooting from a long distance (outside the penalty area).
- Goal shooting contests at close range or in large playing fields.

Correction tips
- Shaking off the opponent by means of dummy runs.
- Running towards the ball and not waiting for it.
- Timely running into the critical zones.
- Shooting at the goal as directly and covertly as possible.
- Accuracy takes precedence over speed.
- When making a solo run at the goal, mislead the goalkeeper into a hasty action by performing a dummy shot at the goal.
- Stay behind the ball and don't forget possible rebounds.

Possible goal shooting techniques
- Kick with the inside of the foot.
- Kick with the full instep.
- Kick with the inside instep.
- Kick with the outside instep.
- Drop kick.
- Hip-turn kick.
- Sideways scissors kick.
- Bicycle kick.
- Kicks with the toe or heel.
- Header.

6.1.3 Learning Systematically How to Shoot at the Goal

Stage 1: Basic drills for beginners
- Shoot a **still** ball directly at the goal.
- Shoot a **rolling** ball directly at the goal.
- Shot at the goal after **controlling a low pass.**

Stage 2: Basic drills for advanced players
Direct shot at the goal of a **low** ball.

Stage 3: 'Double actions'
The players adapt their goal shooting techniques to the situation and to the constantly changing speeds and directions of the ball.

Stage 4: Complex drills
The players shoot at the goal on the run in a **complex drill** (shooting at the goal after passing sequence, pressure of complexity).

Stage 5: Shot at the goal after high ball

The players convert the **thrown ball** with the head or foot. They shoot under difficult conditions (shooting after **turning, sprinting** or **jumping**).

Stage 6: Shooting after tackle

The players shoot at the goal after a **tackle** (opponent pressure).

Stage 7: Shooting under time pressure

The players use goal-shooting techniques under difficult conditions in competitions that simulate time and opponent pressure.

Stage 8: Drills

In odd-sided drills, with neutral players and with equal-sized teams, the players create scoring chances and exploit them while under great pressure from opponents.

6.2   Practical Section

6.2.1   Learning Stage 1: Basic Drills for Beginners

Drills without goalkeeper
The first learning stage involves shooting at an unmanned goal with a still ball.

The players learn to shoot at the goal with the inside of the foot, with the emphasis on accuracy and a clean kicking technique. The coach ensures that the players perform a high number of repetitions. The players kick with the left and right feet from different distances.

6.2.1.1   Shot at the Goal with a Still Ball

Set-up and structure
Set up sufficient target areas (small goals, portable goals, etc.), each player has a ball.

Execution
* Keeping the ball as low as possible, bury it in the back of the net using the inside of the left and right feet.
* The strikers retrieve the balls and get back in line for the next shot.
* 3-5 shots per foot.

Coaching tips
* Place the ball on the ground and take one step back.
* Place the standing leg next to the ball.
* Swing the shooting foot through and run after the ball.

Variations
* Shoot from different distances.
* Small goal scoring contests with still balls simulate time and group pressure.

6.2.1.2   Shooting at the Goal after Dribbling Straight Ahead

Set-up
Set up sufficient target areas and choose the distance of and interval between the cones according to the age and ability of the players, each player has a ball.

Execution
- The players dribble briefly towards the goal and at the second cone kick a low ball into the goal using the inside of the foot.
- The strikers retrieve the ball and dribble to the end of the group.
- 3-5 shots per foot.

Coaching tips
- Dribbling is brief and controlled.
- Place the standing leg next to the ball before kicking it.
- Bring the body's center of gravity forwards.
- Fix the foot, swing the shooting foot through and run after the ball.

6.2.1.3 Turn and Shot

Coaching tips

- Don't turn the ball prematurely, but stay parallel to the dribbling direction until making the shot thus enabling a turn and shot.

- Keep the body's center of gravity forward when shooting.

- Fix the foot, kick the center of the ball and follow the ball (rebound).

Diagonal dribbling

Variations

- Turn and shot away from the goal (270°) and shoot with the other foot.

- Shoot into two different target areas (signal: left, right).

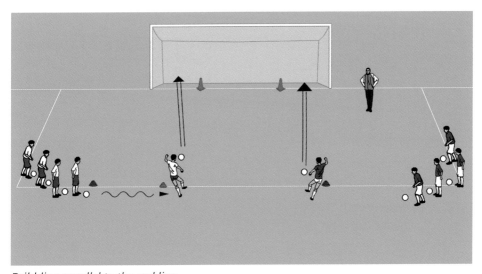

Dribbling parallel to the end line

6.2.1.4   Shot at the Goal after Taking Possession of the Ball

Execution

This is a variation of the turn and shot. The players take possession of the ball from a partner and turn and shoot at the target area.

Coaching tip

The players guide the ball to the far side of the goal and also run with the ball there with the right foot (dribbling with the right foot – run with the ball with the right foot – and vice versa).

6.2.1.5   Shot at the Goal after Diagonal Pass with Ball Control

Set-up

Set up sufficient target areas, with two cones each on the 6 yard line as a boundary line and one cone each for the pass giver on the penalty box line and 1 cone each for the strikers (about 22 yards in front of the goal), the passers of both groups have a ball.

Execution

*   The first striker (A) sprints diagonally, the first passer (B) passes the ball into his path.
*   A receives the ball, runs with it and shoots a low ball from the shooting line with the inside of the foot or the inside instep accurately at goal.
*   The passers stand behind the strikers, then the strikers retrieve their balls and stand behind the passers.

Coaching tips

*   Well-timed passes and clean shooting technique.
*   Confident ball control on the run keeping the ball close to the feet.

6.2.1.6   Shot at the Goal after Square Pass with Ball Control

Set-up
Set up sufficient target areas, two cones each on the 6 yard line as boundaries, two cones each for the passers at the penalty box and two cones for the strikers (about 22 yards in front of the goal), the passers of both groups each have a ball.

Execution
- The first striker (B) sprints diagonally. Halfway to the boundary line, A plays a parallel ball into B's path.
- When level with the shooting line, B kicks an accurate, low ball using the inside of the foot into the previously established target area.
- The passers stand behind the strikers of their group, the strikers retrieve their ball and stand behind the passers. The players change sides after two complete rounds.
- After the first kick from B, C passes the ball to the first striker (D) of the other group.

Observation points
- Timing, length, sharpness and accuracy of the passing.
- Pace and direction of the approaching ball, the strikers' stride length.

6.2.1.7 Shot at the Goal after Back Pass with Ball Control

Set-up
Set up a starting cone for the strikers of each group in the middle of the 18 yard line, two cones as boundary lines at the goal area and 2 target cones in the goal, establish two groups per goal, and each passer has a ball.

Execution
- A2 plays a low pass into the path of the first striker (A1), who sprints away from the starting cone.
- A1 quickly controls the ball briefly, dribbles up to the starting line and shoots the ball as low as possible with the inside of the foot into the established target area, retrieves the ball and goes to stand behind the passers.
- A2 joins the strikers of his group.
- Then the first shooter of group B starts, and so on.
- A round is completed when all players have passed and shot at the goal with both their left and right feet.

Observation points
- Timing, sharpness and accuracy.
- The strikers don't slow down at all directly in front of the goal.
- Short recovery movement of the shooting foot.

6.2.1.8   Shot at the Goal after Long Ball with Ball Control

Set-up
Trapezoid with four cones, the strikers start from the 12-yard point, the passers have a ball each at the penalty area line, and in the goal there are two target areas.

Execution
* The striker (B) runs parallel with the goal line from the starting cone to the second cone.
* Directly before reaching the cone, passer (A) plays a low, accurate and measured pass into B's path.
* The striker quickly controls the ball and shoots on goal keeping the ball as low as possible, retrieves the ball and goes to stand behind the passers, the passers become strikers.

Observation points
* Timing, direction, sharpness and accuracy of passing.
* Safe, quick ball control before shooting.

6.2.1.9 Turn and Shot after Taking the Ball to the Side

Set-up
At the 6 yard box, in a central position in front of the goal, set up a row of cones that represents the area that an opponent behind may cover, two target areas in the goal, passers with balls about 6 yards away in front of the strikers.

Execution
- The striker stands without a ball with his/her back to the goal in front of the center cone.
- The passer plays a low, accurate and measured pass with the inside of the foot.
- Pass the ball if possible with one touch sideways past the row of cones.
- Turn and shot low into the designated target area.
- Striker retrieves the ball and the passer becomes a striker.

Observation points
- The striker should have a slightly open stance and shield the passed ball behind him/her (not go towards it).
- Only goals scored from outside the 6-yard box are valid.

Frequent sources of errors
- Passer doesn't kick the ball hard enough.
- Strikers touch the ball too often, no swivel shot.

Variations
- Receive the ball from the left and right, depending on the pass.
- The passer runs after the ball and puts pressure on the strikers.
- Before receiving the ball, perform a dummy run to the other side.

6.2.2   Learning Stage 2: Basic Drills for Advanced Players

The second learning stage involves the direct conversion of balls that are played low from different directions.

6.2.2.1   Preliminary Drill – Solo Run at Goal

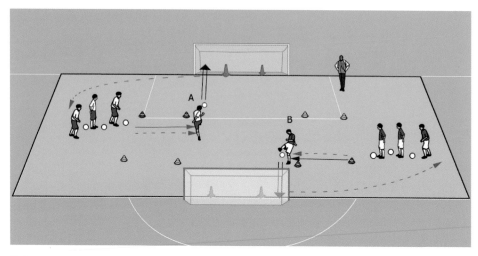

Set-up
One cone level with the post about 6 yards in front of the goal and a starting cone 2-3 yards away, one ball per player.

Execution
The players pass a ball forwards to each other, then perform a turn and shot and bury the ball behind the second cone. This is a very good preliminary drill as strikers are able to determine the timing and pace of the ball themselves.

Variations
- Start from the left and right.
- Start from different directions (deep, diagonal).

6.2.2.2   Direct Shot at the Goal after Diagonal Pass

Set-up

Two target areas, two cones at the shooting line a suitable distance apart (6-1 yards), two cones for the passers at the penalty area and two cones for the strikers (about 22 yards in front of the goal), each passer has a ball.

Execution

- The first striker (A) sprints in fast diagonally, the first passer (B) plays a ball into A's path.
- On reaching the shooting line, A plays an accurate shot at the goal using the inside of the left foot.
- The passers stand behind the strikers; the strikers collect their ball and go to stand behind the passers.
- Repeat with players D and C with the right foot.

Observation points

- Well-timed passes into player's path.
- Clean shooting technique.

Variations

- A second ball (about 2 yards behind the shooting line) is converted directly after the first shot at goal.
- Competition: which group can score the most goals in one round?

6.2.2.3   Direct Shot at the Goal after Square Pass into Player's Path

Set-up
Set up two target areas, two cones on the 6-yard line as boundary lines, two cones for the passers at the penalty area and two cones for the passers at the corners of the penalty area, the passers in both groups each have a ball.

Execution
- The first striker (B1) sprints in diagonally. A passes into B1's path.
- When B1 comes level with the shooting line he plays a low, accurate pass into designated target zone, then the first striker of the other group (D) starts off with the right foot.
- The passers stand behind the strikers of their group; the strikers retrieve their ball and go to stand behind the passers. Change sides after two complete rounds.

Observation points
- Timing, length, sharpness and accuracy of passing.
- Pace and direction of approach to the ball, strikers' stride length.

Variations
- The passers put the strikers under pressure after they pass the ball.
- Group competition: which group can score the most goals in one round?

6.2.2.4 Direct Shot at the Goal after Back Pass from the Goal Line

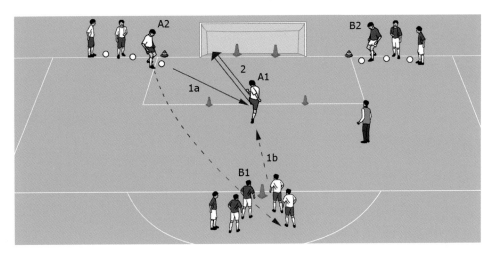

Set-up

In the goal there are two target areas, set up one starting cone for the strikers of each group in the middle of the edge of the penalty box, 2 passing cones on the goal line near the 6 yard box and two cones as shooting lines about 6 yards in front of the goal, the passers of each group get a ball.

Execution

* The first striker (A1) sprints from the starting cone and receives a flat back pass from A2.
* The player runs straight towards the ball and buries it as flatly as possible with the inside of the foot in a target area, retrieves the ball and goes to stand behind the passers.
* A2 now becomes the striker of the group.
* Next the first striker of group B starts, etc.
* A round is completed when all players have passed and scored once with both left and right feet.

Observation points

* Timing, sharpness and passing accuracy.
* The striker must not slow down immediately before shooting at the goal.
* Short recovery movement of the shooting foot.

Variations

* The passers dribble to the touchline before playing a back pass.
* Group competition: which group scores more goals in one round?

6.2.2.5   Direct Shot at the Goal after Long Ball into Player's Path

Set-up

A trapezoid with four cones, the goalkeepers start level with the 12-yard box, the passers each have a ball at the edge of the penalty box edge, there are two target areas in the goal.

Execution

- The striker (B) runs parallel to the goal line from the starting cone to the second cone.
- Just before he/she reaches the cone, passer A plays a flat, accurate and measured pass into B's path.
- The striker plays a direct, low shot at the goal, retrieves the ball and goes to stand behind the passers, while the passers become strikers.

Observation points

- Timing, direction, sharpness and accuracy of passes.
- Precise, direct shooting at the goal.

6.2.2.6   Direct Turn and Shot after Pass

Set-up
A row of cones is set up in a central position in front of the goal, representing the space covered by an imaginary opponent behind, two target areas in the goal, one cone for the passer in a central position about 6 yards in front of the goalkeeper.

Execution
- The striker stands without a ball with his/her back to the goal in front of the middle cone.
- The passer plays a low, accurate and measured ball with the inside of the foot to the left or right.
- The striker sprints to the ball and turns and shoots low into the designated target area.
- The striker retrieves the ball and the passer becomes a striker.

Observation points
- Direction, sharpness and accuracy of passes.
- Precision when shooting at the goal.

6.2.3   Learning Stage 3: Double Action

6.2.3.1   **Double Action 1**

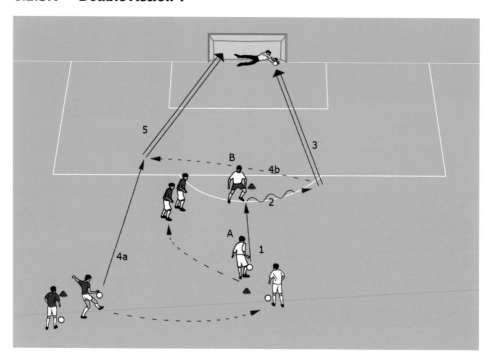

Set-up
Playing field is double the penalty area, one goal with goalkeeper, striker at the penalty area edge, passer at the center and lateral cones.

Execution
A plays a ball to player B (1), who brings the ball under control while turning towards the goal (2) and shoots at the goal with the goalkeeper (3). Then B sprints to the side and exploits a ball passed to him/her by the passer B standing at the side (4a, 4b).

Variation
*   The passer follows his/her pass and acts as a defender in order to place the striker under pressure.

6.2.3.2 Double Action 2

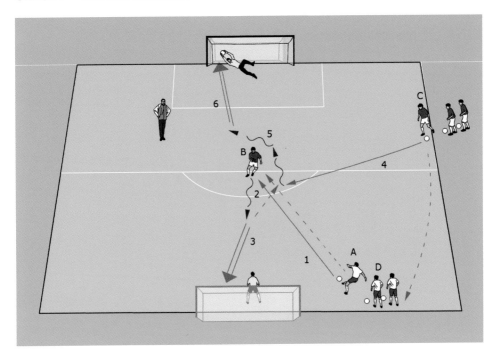

Set-up
Playing field: doubled penalty area, number of players: 10-14 and two goalkeepers, 8-12 balls, two goals, passer 1 at the side next to the goal, passer 2 to the side level with the half-way line.

Execution
A passes to B and takes over his/her position. B dribbles to the first goal (2) and shoots at goal (3) and sprints to the other side to receive a pass from C (4), controls it and shoots at the other goal (5). Then B stands in C's position and A waits for the pass from D. C takes over A's position.

Coaching tips
- Fast double action followed by shot at the goal.
- Variations with and without goalkeeper.
- Passers sprint after ball and tackle the strikers.

6.2.4 Learning Stage 4: Complex Drills

6.2.4.1 Direct Pass in Square with Shot at the Goal (1)

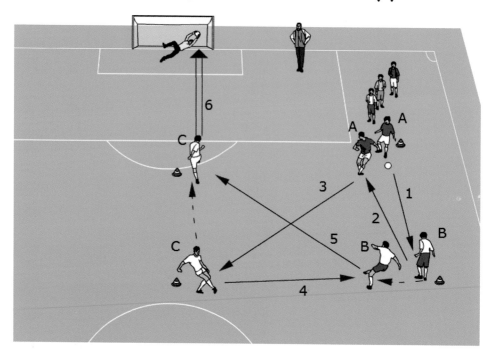

Set-up
A square beyond the penalty area, 8-10 outfield players and a goalkeeper in the large goal, two players without a ball at the free cones, the other players with balls at the starting cones.

Execution
A passes to B and makes him/herself free at the side to receive a pass, B passes back to A and immediately makes him/herself available for a give and go with C, A passes diagonally to C and then takes B's place, C plays a give and go with B and sprints to the next cone, B 'drips' the ball to C and takes C's place, C sprints to the ball and shoots at the goal (directly or after quickly controlling the ball). Finally C retrieves the ball and dribbles to the end of the group.

Coaching tip
If the number of players is too big (more than 10 players), split the group in two and add another goal to reduce waiting times at the start and give the players more shots at the goal, i.e. more repetitions and a more successful learning process.

6.2.4.2　Direct Pass in Square with Shot at the Goal (2)

Set-up
A square outside the penalty box, 8-10 outfield players and a goalkeeper in the large goal, two players without a ball at the free cones, the other players with a ball at the starting cone.

Execution
A passes to B and quickly makes him/herself free to the side. B passes back to A and immediately prepares him/herself for a give and go with C, A passes diagonally to C and then takes B's place, C plays a give and go with B and sprints to the ball that B passes diagonally into his/her path, B passes into C's path and takes C's place, C finishes with a shot at the goal (directly or after quickly controlling the ball).

Coaching tip
The nature of the task changes for the players if the passing sequence is rotated by 90 degrees. The start of the drill is now the diagonally opposite corner. The strikers don't start perpendicular to the goalkeeper but parallel to the penalty box edge, thus enabling the players to practice the turn and shot. If the start is to the right of the goal, the strikers train their left foot and vice versa.

6.2.4.3 One-Two with Shot at the Goal

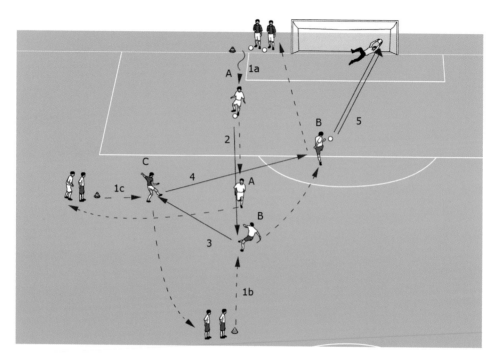

Set-up

Players with a ball stand at a starting cone 6 yards from the goal, 2-3 players at a cone about 33 yards away and 2-3 players at a cone to the side level with the penalty box.

Execution

Player A dribbles towards B, about 6 yards in front of him he plays a pass to B, sprints up to him and attacks him. B plays a one-two with C, shoots at the goal and goes to stand at the end of group A. A runs to group C and C takes B's place..

Variations

• Pass to the other side (one-two to the right).
• Vary the gaps between the cones.

Coaching tips

• If the attacking player is still too far away, the striker quickly accepts the ball before the one-two and plays the pass to the side when the player is close enough.
• Dribbling with a faked pass to the side is also possible.
• If the one-two is not played accurately, the striker quickly controls the ball before shooting at the goal.

6.2.5   Learning Stage 5: Shot at the Goal after High Ball

The difficulty increases if the balls preceding the shot at the goal are played high (either throws or passes). The strikers shoot at the goal directly or after controlling the ball. Players must train specifically for both.

Sequence:
- Preliminary drill: shot at the goal after **self-thrown ball.**
- Shot at the goal after **ball thrown by partner** (convert with head or feet).
- Shot at the goal **after high ball** (e.g. cross).

6.2.5.1   Preliminary Drill: Drop Kick and Frontal Volley

Set-up
2 target areas in the goal, two starting cones level with the 6-yard box and three other cones about 2 yards away. Players stand holding the ball in their hands behind the other cones.

Execution
- The first two strikers drop their ball with both hands at the 6-yard line and play

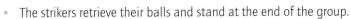

a drop-kick on goal using the full instep.
- The strikers retrieve their balls and stand at the end of the group.

Coaching tips
- The ball should be kicked low and hard.
- The ball should not be kicked too far away from the body, the center of gravity should be as far as possible over the ball, the toes point to the ground when the ball is kicked, the shooting foot should not swing through too high.

6.2.5.2   Hip Turn Shot

Set-up
Two target areas in the goal, two starting cones about 1-2 yards to the sides of the goal posts, each player has a ball.

Execution
- The first strikers stand with their upper bodies at right angles to the goal line and drop the ball to the ground.
- They kick the high bouncing ball with a hip turn shot with as straight a trajectory as possible at mid-height into the designated target areas.
- The strikers retrieve their balls and go to stand at the opposite starting cone.
- Once the target areas are free, the next strikers start.

Coaching tips
- The swinging direction of the shooting foot is back to front, not bottom to top.
- The turning movement starts as the ball is kicked in the center towards the goal with an extended foot.

6.2.5.3 Shot at the Goal from Thrown Ball (with Foot or Head)

Set-up
The striker stands near the 12-yard box, the throwers are spread out in the penalty area and have one ball each, one goalkeeper in a normal goal.

Execution
The striker converts the balls thrown from different directions after quickly controlling the ball.

Variation
Convert thrown balls directly with head or feet.

6.2.5.4   Shot at the Goal from High Ball

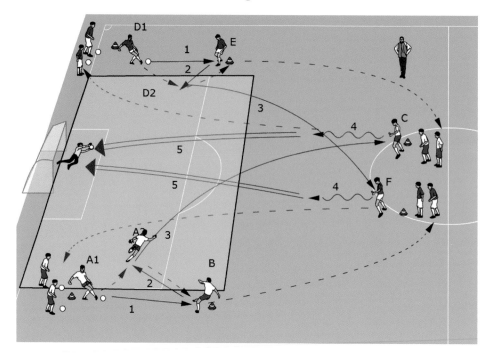

Set-up
2 groups of strikers wait about 27 – 33 yards away from the goal. The groups stand 9-11 yards apart, two passers (B and E) stand at the corners of the penalty area, 7-9 yards away are the starting players (A and D) with a ball.

Execution
After playing a give and go with B, A passes a high ball diagonally to C, who quickly controls the ball and takes it towards the goal. From the predetermined distance (e.g., the edge of the penalty area), C shoots at the goal. Then the same procedure is performed on the other side, started by D, via E to F. The give and go players run to the end of the goal shooting group and the strikers to the end of the starting group.

Variations
* Vary the gap between the goal shooting groups and the goal.
* Introduce opponents in front of the penalty area.

6.2.6   Learning Stage 6: Shot at the Goal after Tackle

6.2.6.1   Shot at the Goal after Tackle (1)

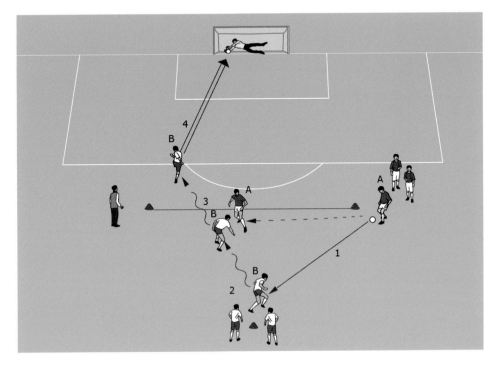

Set-up
Doubled penalty area, one goal with goalkeeper, three cones, 5-10 balls depending on the number of players.

Execution
Defender A passes to attacker B, who tries to dribble over the line. A attacks sideways and tries to stop B. After successfully dribbling over the line, B can shoot at goal without pressure.

Coaching tips
- Fast and purposeful ball control.
- Dribbling with changes of direction and feints when opponent attacks.
- Accurate shot at goal after dribbling over the line.

6.2.6.2   Shot at the Goal after Tackle (2)

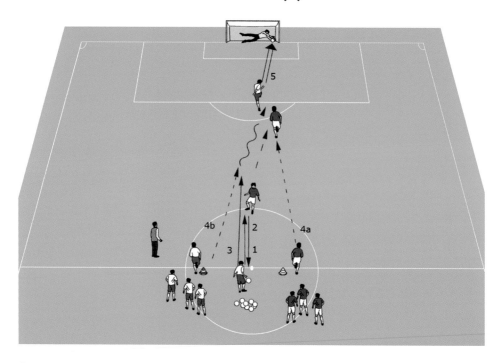

Set-up
Start at the halfway line, one goal with goalkeeper, players wait in pairs next to two starting cones.

Execution
Two neutral players pass a ball to each other. The player with his/her back to the goal suddenly lets the ball roll toward the goal between their legs, thus initiating the tackle of the two first players of each group around the ball. The player who is fighting for the ball acts as attacker and the other player as defender.

Variations
* Vary the distance between the passers and sprinters and to the goal.
* Team competition: which team scores most goals.

6.2.6.3   Shot at the Goal after Tackle (3)

Set-up
Doubled penalty area, two goals with goalkeepers, one pass from the baseline and second pass in the middle of the playing area.

Execution
A passes to B and attacks him/her (1). B dribbles up to A, passes him/her with a feint (2) shoots at the goal (3). B sprints to the other side and receives a pass from C (4), who also attacks him/her from the side. B controls the second ball and shoots under pressure at the other goal (5). B then stands in position C and A waits for a pass from D.

Observation points
* Fast double action followed by shot at the goal.
* Use of different feints.
* The opponent's efforts should correspond to the attacker's ability.

6.2.7 Learning Stage 7: Shot at the Goal under Time Pressure

How can match pressure be simulated in training?

In competitive games, players rarely have time to prepare perfectly for a shot at the goal and to think through the shooting action.

Everything moves very fast and is usually automatic. This time, accuracy and group pressure can be reproduced very well in small goal shooting competitions. Under time pressure, the players shoot precisely at targets or try to score in small matches where they learn to score even under pressure.

Goal scoring competitions

Goal scoring competitions are very motivating for players. The accuracy and group pressure also simulate the game situation.

The players use what they have learned in drills in small competitions and games. Only when they can quickly and confidently score a goal under match pressure has goal shooting training been successful.

6.2.7.1 Cone Kicking

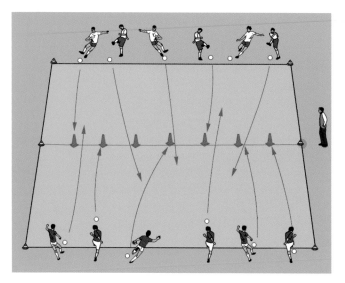

Set-up

Two teams stand on two lines about 16-22 yards away from each other. A row of cones is placed in the middle. Each player starts with a ball.

Execution
- The players try to kick the cones from their lines.
- They may kick all the balls that are on their side.
- The playing field may only be entered briefly in order to retrieve a ball.

Competition
- Play until all cones have been hit.
- Which team can hit the most cones in a given time?

Variations
- Put the cones on a bench.

6.2.7.2   Kicking Balls Off Cones

Set-up

Two teams stand at two lines about 16 yards away from each other. A row of cones is set up in between them with balls on top of them. Each player starts off with a ball.

Execution
- The players try to kick the balls off the cones from their lines.
- They may kick all the balls that are on their side.
- The playing field may only be entered briefly in order to retrieve a ball.

Competition
- Play until all cones have been hit.
- Which team can score the most hits in a given time?

6.2.7.3   Passing Sequence with Shot at the Goal

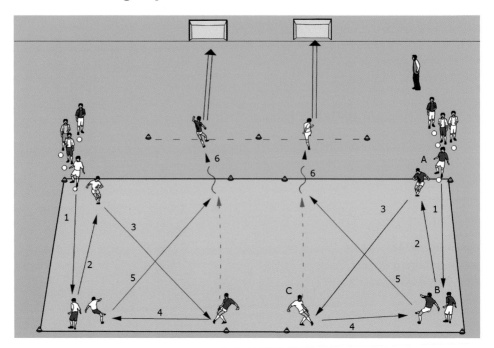

Set-up
Two groups with about 6-8 players each have a square, a target area and a mini-goal and 4-6 balls.

Execution
- In this competition, the players shoot into a mini goal after a predetermined passing sequence (forward – backward – diagonally – square) before the shooting line.
- The striker quickly retrieves his/her ball from the goal and stands behind the last player of his group.
- Each team starts once from the left and once from the right.
- Add up the goals scored.

Coaching tips
- The distance to the goal depends on the players' ability.
- The aim is to pass or shoot at the goal cleanly despite the time pressure.
- The players learn to ensure a balance between speed and precision (accuracy takes precedence over speed!), as they want to score as many goals as possible and win the game.

6.2.7.4   3v1 + 1 from Behind

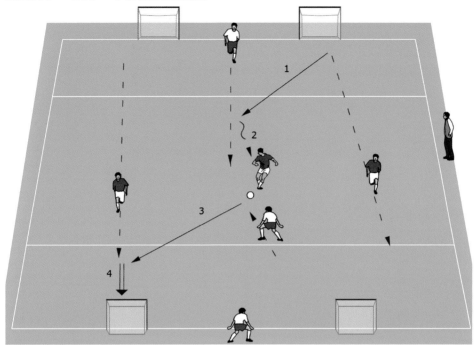

Set-up
Playing area: about 27 x 37 yards, four mini goals, groups of three players and one ball.

Execution
- Play 3 against 1.
- With the first touch of the ball by a striker, another defender joins in, and stands 2-3 yards behind the strikers.
- The third defender has a rest and is substituted off at the next attack. He waits behind the starting line.

Coaching tips
- It is difficult for the attackers when not only the distance but also the starting position of the additional defenders change. They have to spot this and adapt their game to the new situation.
- Avoid unnecessary passes that do not gain space.
- The last pass takes place when the defender joins in (ideally directly before the action space of the opposing player).
- The attacker in possession of the ball takes into account the defender's behavior, the direction in which the second defender is running and the receiving position of both his teammates.

6.2.7.5   3v1 + 2 from Behind

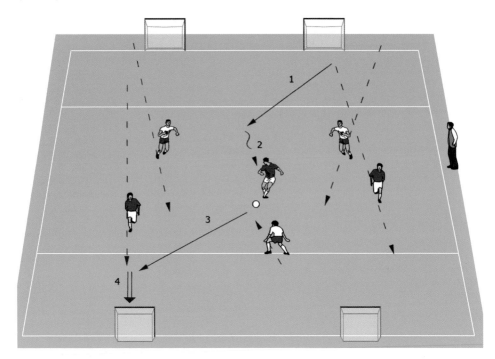

Set-up
Playing area: about 27 x 37 yards, four mini goals, groups of three players, one ball.

Execution
Play 3 against 1. Two other defenders join in to put the attackers under pressure. Depending on their age and ability, they start between 2 and 3 yards behind the attackers and try to gain possession of the ball.

Coaching tips
* The pressure on the attacker increases when the defender is aided by two additional defenders. This competition trains the ability of the players to pass the ball even more quickly and accurately, to run into a free space and score goals when they are under time pressure and hard pressed by defenders.
* The positions of the defenders must change constantly so that the attackers improve their perception and learn to adapt their attacking play to the behavior of the defenders.

6.2.8   Learning Stage 8: Game Forms

Introduction

The best shooting technique in the world is useless if the players are not able to exploit the ball under great spatial, opponent and time pressure in a complex game situation. That is why game-specific goal scoring training must simulate match pressure, as far as this can be done in training. Game forms involving shooting at the goal in a doubled penalty area are particularly well-suited to this. The players learn to anticipate extremely quickly, i.e. to spot, prepare for and exploit scoring chances.

Most goals are the product of a first or second touch ball inside the penalty area. The technical perfection of the first touch shot at the goal and the perfect ball control at the first touch should be the principle objective of modern goal shooting training. An accurate last pass (the 'deadly pass') to the strikers is also vital.

Increasing difficulty

Opponent pressure should be increased gradually. It is a good idea to start with odd-sided game forms. Use either odd-sided fixed teams are formed (e.g. 8v4) or include neutral players (e.g. 4v4 + 4 neutral players).

The team numbers are then evened out, thus increasing the pressure on the attackers until finally matches take place with even-sided teams.

6.2.8.1 2v1 with Small Goals
(Odd-sided Game Form from Youth Soccer)

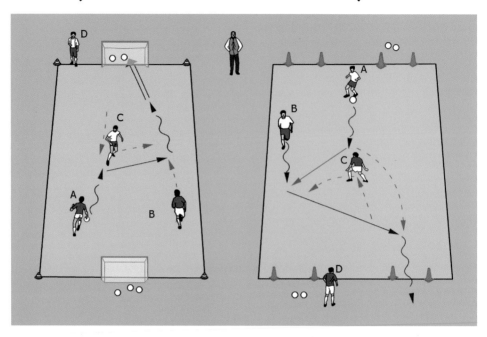

Set-up
Playing area about 11 x 16 yards, groups of two players, max. playing time two minutes.

Execution
- A and B play 2 against 1 against C, D rests to start with.
- If the larger team scores a goal, the striker leaves the field and stands behind his goal.
- D then plays 2v1 with C.
- The player in the team of one can score goals alone, only if the team of two scores a goal does the number of players change.
- Which team scores the most goals in five minutes?

Learning objectives
- The basics of purposeful team play (running into free space, timing of passes).
- Shooting at the goal under opponent pressure.
- Offensive and defensive tackling.

6.2.8.2   4v2 with 1 Goal

Set-up
Playing area: penalty area, four attackers, two defenders, one goalkeeper.

Execution
- The four attackers start attacking from the edge of the penalty area and try to shoot at the goal as frequently and effectively as possible by passing to each other.
- If possession of the ball is lost, the ball is miskicked or held, the player responsible changes places with the defender who has been playing the longest.

Coaching tips
- After a completed attack, the goalkeeper rolls or throws the ball to one of the outfielders.
- If an attacker makes a mistake, the players concerned quickly swap marking vests.

Variations
The ratio of attackers to defenders can be varied in many ways. The coach sets up the odd-sided teams so that the attackers can shoot at the goal as often as possible.

The stronger the attackers, the smaller the difference in team size.
- 4v1 (easier for the attackers).
- 4v3 (harder for the attackers).
- 5v2.
- 5v3.
- 6v4.

6.2.8.3 4v1 Goal Scoring Game with Long-range Shots

Set-up
Playing area: doubled penalty area, two goals with goalkeeper, two teams of four players each.

Execution
Goals are only valid if scored from the team's own half (shots outside the penalty area). Four players from the attacking team play against one player who tackles inside the opposing team's half. If the tackling player wins the ball, he/she passes it to his/her teammates in their own half.

Coaching tips
- The defending team should block the shooting path by cleverly shifting around.
- The tackling player should change constantly.

6.2.8.4   4v4 + 4 Pass Receivers with One Goal

Set-up
Playing area: extended penalty area, one goal with goalkeeper, three teams of four players.

Execution
Two teams A and B play 4 against 4 on the playing area. The four players from team C position themselves as pass receivers around the field. After possession of the ball has been won, an outfielder must be passed to before he may start another attack on goal. All the players play against each other: A against B, A against C, B against C.

Playing time: 5 minutes.

Variations
• Limit the number of ball touches (one touch only with the outside of the foot, two touches with the inside of the foot).
• Goals after inter-team passing with an outfielder are worth double (triple) points.

6.2.8.5   4 + 4v4 + 4 in Doubled Penalty Area

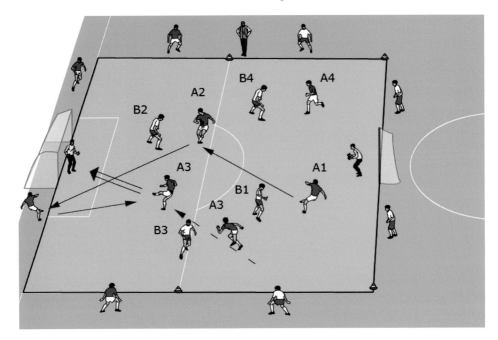

Set-up
Doubled penalty area, 4v4 in the field, two players from each team stand behind the opposing goal, two players on the touchline of the opposing team's half.

Execution
The teams play 4v4 in the doubled 16-yard area. The teams' own outfielders are spread out evenly behind the halfway line. The outfielders are not allowed to pass to each other.

Variations
* 4v4 + 2 neutral players behind the goal.
* 4v4 + 2 neutral players on the touchlines.
* Long-range balls from the teams' own halves are worth double points.
* Outfielders can pass between each other.
* Limit the number of touches for the infield players (three, two or one touches).
* A goal is only valid if at least one outfielder takes part in the attack.

Coaching tips
* The game encourages one-twos.
* The outfielders next to the goals encourage long balls.

6.2.8.6 Passes to Four Goals in a Cross Formation

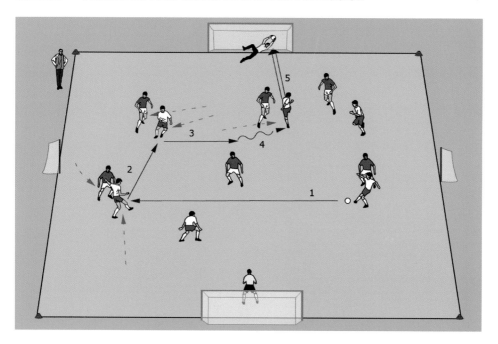

Set-up

Playing area about 33 x 33 yards, four goals (small goals, post goals, normal goals), two teams, two or four goalkeepers.

Execution

- The red team attacks both goals (next to each other) that are defended by the blue team.
- The offside rule does not apply.

Learning objectives

- Purposeful shots at the goal under opponent pressure from typical match distances.
- Set up and successfully win 2 on 1 situations.
- Shifts of attack and fast changes of direction after losing the ball.
- Cognitive, decision-making and reaction abilities.

Variations

- 3v3 plus goalkeeper.
- 4v4 plus goalkeeper.
- 5v5 plus goalkeeper.

FINAL COMMENTS

- Perfect ball control should never be an end in itself, but always be seen in the context of a game situation and an opponent. Only purposeful and tactically smart behavior before, during and after the first touch of the ball is helpful for the team as a whole.

- Always take the ages and abilities of your players into account when selecting exercises, drills and game forms.

- Be patient when introducing new techniques (juggling, flicks) and motivate your players to practice in their own spare time. Club practice times are not enough to automate difficult movement sequences.

- The drills and training content presented in this book should be seen as a stimulus to further study. Be creative and develop your own variations and your personal training concept.

Let me remind you once more:

Your teams are more likely to play successful and creative soccer if players are able to bring the ball under control quickly, safely and on the run in the most difficult situations. The slightest ball control error is immediately punished by the loss of possession of the ball. Only perfect ball control enables players to cope with the demands of modern soccer.

Good luck when trying out and varying the featured drills; I hope you will find them useful in your coaching work.

Yours, Peter Schreiner

BOOKS

Bidzinski, M. (2004). Soccer: *Smart First Touches, Developing the Skillful Player*, Spring City: Reedswain.

Bruggemann, D. (1989). *Kinder- und Jugendtraining, Fußball-Handbuch 2*, Schondorf: Hofmann-Verlag.

Häfelinger, U., Schuba, V. (2002). *Propriozeptives Training*, Aachen: Meyer & Meyer.

Hirtz, P./Hotz, A./Ludwig, G. (2000). *Praxisideen 2, Bewegungskompetenzen, Koordinationstherapie – Gleichgewicht*, Schondorf: Hofmann-Verlag.

Hughes, Ch. (1990). *The Winning Formula, Soccer Skills and Tactics*, London: Collins.

Meyer, R. (2001). *Torschusstraining Fußball*, Reinbek: Rowolt-Verlag.

Hübscher, S. (2006). Creative and Successful Wing Play, Institute for Youth Soccer, Germany.

Elgert, N./Schreiner, P. (2005). One Touch & Combination Play, Part 1, Institute for Youth Soccer, Germany.

Elgert, N./Schreiner, P. (2005). One Touch & Combination Play, Part 2, Institute for Youth Soccer, Germany.

Elgert, N./Schreiner, P. (2006). *Moderner Angriffsfußball,* Reinbek: Rowolt-Verlag.

Schreiner, P. (2000). *Koordinationstraining Fußball*, Reinbek: Rowolt-Verlag.

Schreiner, P. (2001). *Kinder- und Jugendtraining*, die besten Trainingseinheiten, Reinbek: Rowolt-Verlag.

Wein, H. (2000). *Developing Youth Soccer Players, Coaching with the Better Soccer Development Model*, Leeds, Human Kinetics.

Wein, H. (2004). *Developing Game Intelligence in Soccer*, Spring City: Reedswain.

DVDS

P. Schreiner/Dr. G. Thissen (2009). Coordination Training for Soccer – Balance, the key to perfect ball handling, Institute for Youth Soccer, Germany.

N. Elgert/ P. Schreiner (2004) The Art of Playing Offensive, Part 1 + 2, Institute for Youth Soccer, Germany.

Schreiner, P. (2007). The Creative Dribbler; Institute for Youth Soccer, Germany.

Schreiner, P. (2008). SOCCER - Perfect Ball Mastery, Institute for Youth Soccer, Germany.

Photo & Illustration Credits

Photos: Dr. Marion Becker-Richter
p. 14: © Michael Flippo, fotolia.com / p. 40: © kristian sekulic, fotolia.com / p. 52: © Ian MacLellan, fotolia.com/ p. 120: © Andreas Gradin, fotolia.com / p. 148: © Andreas Gradin, fotolia.com / p. 160: © sportgraphic, fotolia.com / p. 204: © Michael Flippo, fotolia.com

Graphics: Nils Huber
Cover design: Sabine Groten, Aachen
Cover photos: © olly, fotolia.com

The soccer diagrams were created with easy Sports-Graphics (www.sports-graphics.com).